Lectures on Korean ODA and Law

LECTURES ON KOREAN ODA AND LAW

Official Development Assistance

BONGCHUL KIM · HO KIM

HU:iNE

Lectures on Korean ODA and Law
by *Bongchul Kim, Ho Kim*

Cover design by EwhanD&B (+82-2-2254-4301)
Edited by Sunho Shin, Inwoo Choi, and EwhanD&B
Printed by SJC Sung Jeon (+82-31-955-8800)

Published in Republic of Korea by Huine, an imprint of Hankuk University of Foreign Studies University Knowledge Press, Seoul.
http://press.hufs.ac.kr

First printing, July 20th, 2016

ISBN 979-11-5901-066-8 93360
Price 18,000 Won

Preface

Preface

Official Development Assistance (ODA) is aiming to arrive at development-cooperation with the hands of nations, governments, and international organizations. Therefore, such activities are originally regarded as 'public activity' in which national taxes or public assets are used. However, collaboration with corporations, citizens, and NGOs can make other huge effects on ODA activities. In fact, although such activities tend to make close relations to politics or economics, we have to remember that it is also based on laws, according to the 'rule of law' concepts treating social activities. International ODA institutions and their businesses are closely related to international laws and when it is connected to domestic society, it starts to make relationship with domestic laws. So for an accurate understanding of ODA, and more outstanding performances learning related laws and making best use of them shall be necessary.

The Republic of Korea has built a reputation for an area of International Development Cooperation and ODA. Since the Korean War starting from the 1950s, international assistance to Korea has transformed into various ways, and played a key role to industrialization and widening trade. Along with it, it has also influenced economic development of Korea in 1970~80's. And now, from the year of 2000, as a donor country Korea has been trying to share its experience of economic development to international societies. And for the understanding of Korean ODA, we have to look back on international laws and domestic laws related to its activities.

This book is to provide the understandings of the various aspects in ODA, or international development cooperation area to students. For it, I organized all materials from lectures including ODA and laws and ODA and trade for the Division of International studies and the Graduate School of International And Area Studies in Hankuk University of Foreign Studies. This is constituted the contents with an amount of half-year semester. I'd like to apologize because there is not much universities who provide ODA and law lectures in a regular basis in their academic courses, but with this book I hope that all of you will widen your view of ODA and related laws. Hopefully, it might be a tool for the better understanding of Korea, which has a unique position in international society.

Editor

Contents

Lecture 10. International Law for the Korean ODA Works • 215

Lecture 11. Domestic Laws for the Korean ODA • 233

Lecture 12. The Law for KOICA • 261

Lecture 1. Introduction to the Study and Basic Points of the 'ODA'

1. The Objectives of the Class

2. International Development and ODA

3. Basic Points of the 'ODA'

Introduction to the Study and Basic Points of the 'ODA'

1. The Objectives of the Class

• Basic information about the issue

The word of 'Development' means 'the process of developing or being developed' or 'an event constituting a new stage in a changing situation'. The United Nations Development Programme (UNDP) defines that 'Development' is about expanding the choices people have to lead lives that they value. Then, they use the definition in many fields. For example, they develop economically something to increase income or provide better housing, clothing, food, work or leisure. Development can be done in the field of politics for the improvement of democracy or good governance (better public service). Sometimes the works of development are for the justice or equality (non-discrimination:

race, gender, nationality, localism, nepotism, etc.) in a society. Recently, many developments are done even for the better environment (such as health, clean water, air and greens).

The development works are normally done in the international stage (international development) and they naturally need international cooperation. The first step of the study is an Introduction to the International Development and Cooperation issues. It is based on the understandings of The Theories and The International Relationships.

The legal issues in the International Society are covered by International Laws. Therefore, the legal issues on international development works in the international society are also covered by International Laws. The category of the international laws is 'International Development Law'. Through studying International Development Laws, some rules can be established as ideal models for the regulation of governments and organizations in the international society.

• Key Facts

In order to be able to study the international development laws, some facts or principles in the international stage, such as the SDGs of the UN, must be considered. These points are directly related to the laws and the International organizations such as MDBs and NGOs. These laws are also based on the background and concepts on the issues.

• Korea's position

Recently, the Korean development works have become important in the international society. These recent developmental works are based on the experience and history of Korea. Can we develop the Korean Style within this international field? Of course, it must be regulated by the Korean development laws; therefore, building 'The Korean Models or Policies' in this area is naturally influenced by the International and National Laws of the issue.

2. International Development and ODA

• Definitions and Origins

The definition of 'International Development' is development work for a greater quality of life for humans. It is 'Human development work on a Global level'. There are some universal meanings but no universally accepted definitions. This work is directly related to 'International Aid' and 'Humanitarian Aid'. The meaning of international development in Modern History has changed. Development has always been an issue for every country. Ideas of development were considered as synonyms of prosperity and often misunderstood as solutions to various problems. Since the concept of development is so vague, each actor had different methods. On behalf of the world, developed countries decided to form international organizations and volunteered to spread the way of 'development.' This definition has, for 40 years, been the global standard for measuring donor efforts in supporting developmental cooperation objectives.

The concept originated from colonialism. The colonization or globalization of developing countries by some developed countries is justified under the name of 'Development'. The establishment of new free trade policies between 'developed' and 'underdeveloped' nations is also related to this concept. Sometimes, reconstruction works post World War II has been influenced by the concepts. During the Cold War period, the US friendly groups and the former Soviet friendly groups were also managed by the concepts for the ideological rivalry.

• Changing concepts

The concept of the 'development work' has been changed from the 'Modernisation' or 'Structural adjustment' to 'Poverty reduction'. Originally, the concept was used for the social and economical structural transformations as part of the development, creating industrialisation and intentional industrial policies. However, the concept has changed to the 'Direct budget support for social welfare programmes' that create macroeconomic stability leading to an increase in economic growth.

• Criticisms of concepts in International Development

There are many critical opinions on the development works. For example, one opinion insists that the world distribution of wealth is much more unequal than that of income. Some developed countries are trying to inject the concept of 'development for developed countries' into developing countries with lingering effects of colonialism, fundamentally known 'neo-colonial'. Some developed countries may use force to apply their industrial and economic structure on poorer countries making the consumers in poor countries poorer under the name of the development.

• Official Development Assistance (ODA)

In the works of International Development, some governmental (Public) actions from the central and/or local governments of donor countries and multilateral agencies to developing countries (the recipient country) for the promotion of the economic development and for the improvement of the quality of life in developing countries, can be categorized as Official Development Assistance (ODA). It is the flow of financial resources to developing countries providing 'grants' or 'concessional loans'. ODA deals with financial resources provided by the central and local governments of donating countries. These public works are provided by official agencies, including state and local governments, or by their executive agencies. It can moreover be founded in multilateral agencies consisting of a group of donating countries such as the G20 for example.

< International Development works and ODA >

There are two types of main methods in ODA action. 'Grant' is a free form of assistance through cash, goods, and/or services. A donor country provides a grant aid without stipulations of repayment or redemption. 'Concessional Loan' is a type of funding provided either in cash or goods. A donor country may provide it with stipulations of liabilities for repayment. Although this type of aid requires repayment, it is more favourable to the recipient country than other commercially available loans in terms of interest rates, maturity, and grace periods. In order to count as ODA, a concessional loan type must have a grant element of 25% or more.

< The Flow of ODAs >

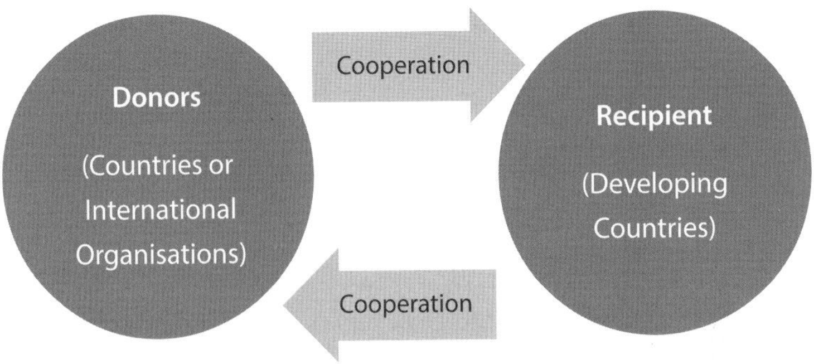

3. Basic Points of the 'ODA'

• Main directions of ODA

ODA work is mainly categorized under several directions as discussed below;.

< The main directions of ODA >

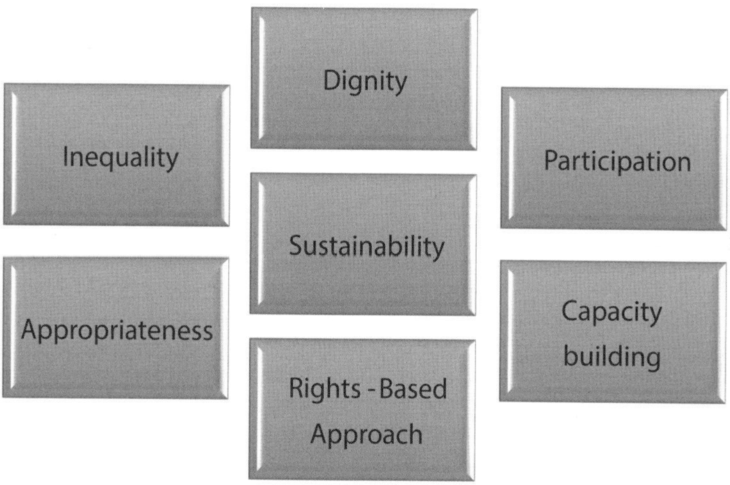

ODA works must be based on the recognition of the 'inequalities' within a nation and between nations. The first article of 'Universal Declaration of Human Rights' states "all human beings are born free and equal in dignity and rights", providing another direction: 'Dignity'. ODA work must be based on the concept of 'Participation', ensuring that the intended beneficiaries of development projects and programmes actively take part in their own development. Any kind of ODA project must be done under the 'appropriateness', which considers correct scale and technical level. That means good ODA work is culturally and socially suitable for its beneficiaries.

'Sustainability' is also an important point. Sustainable business practices lead to economic growth and the empowerment of the recipient country, removing the dependency on overseas aid. Increasing the ability of the recipients is 'Capacity building' to continue their future development alone, without external support. This is a parallel concept to sustainability. Combining many different concepts of international development, such as capacity building, participation and sustainability, the 'Rights-Based Approach' is empowering the rights-holders who do not exercise full rights and strengthening the capacity of the duty-bearers to fulfil the rights.

• The main fields of ODA

Many ODA projects are done within a variety of fields such as Foreign aid, Governance, Healthcare and Education. Of course, some traditional issues such as Poverty reduction, Economics and Infrastructure are still the main fields of developmental work. Recently, Gender equality, Disaster preparedness, Human rights and Environment are also becoming important fields of ODA projects. These ODA fields are directly related and interact with each other.

< Interaction between fields >

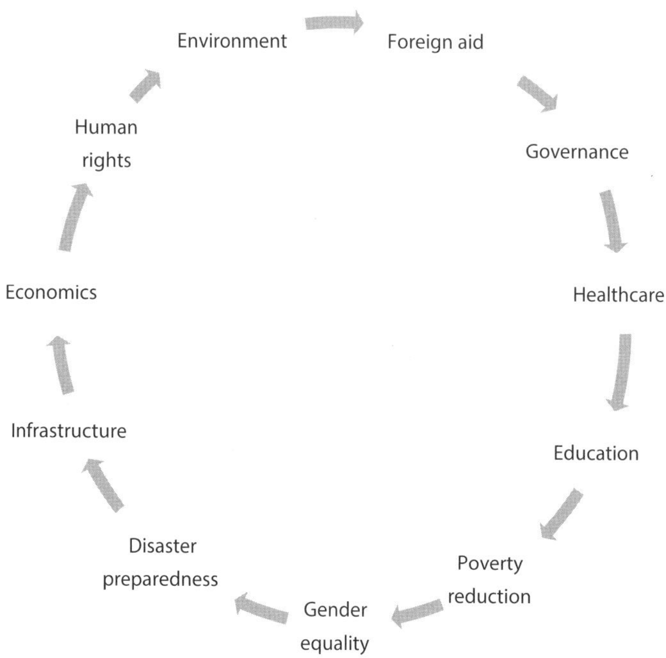

• Practice of ODAs

ODA projects are practiced in many different ways. 'Measurement' is judging how developed a country or what further development is necessary or desirable, such as National GDP, Literacy rates, Life expectancy, Per capita income, Maternal survival rate, HIV infection rates, and Number of doctors per capita. 'Migration' is leading to significant international development. For example, Culture, knowledge, skills and technologies can be developed with the move of people.

'Water and sanitation' is one important theme of developmental practice, which is the water and sanitary provision (such as toilets, bathing facilities) of sufficient quantity and quality. They can be related to the provision of access to quality 'healthcare' to the population in an efficient and consistent manner. This ODA work requires chellenging engineering aspects, such as infrastructure (hospitals and transport systems) and education challenges (qualified health-workers and educated consumers).

'Education' projects firstly focus on providing free primary level education, but they also cover secondary and higher education. Almost every development project includes an aspect of education, such as building a school, providing teachers and their training. 'Shelter' is providing suitable housing for families and communities. This is more specified to the context of culture, location, climate and other factors. 'Human rights' issues are recently emerging within stage of ODA practice. Many ODA works deal with provisions of International human rights instruments. There are also many international development projects including rights associated with gender equality, justice, employment, social welfare and culture.

'Livelihood' is ensuring that all people are able to make a living for themselves and provide themselves with an adequate standard of living. 'Finance' issues are important for the long run ODA effects and economic growth of the recipient country. These developmental works mainly provide financial systems and frameworks for their own development, and sometimes ODA projects are practiced in microfinance and so called 'Right-financing'.

Lecture 2. Paradigm of the Development in the International Society

1. Prospects of International Development and ODA
2. New Paradigms for the Development Activities in the International Society
3. Other Systems

Paradigm of the Development in the International Society

1. Prospects of International Development and ODA

As the previous lecture has shown, there have been various efforts on development issues in the international society, especially after World War II, when the world felt the need for peace and cooperation. With the progress of discourse on the issues, international actors discussed the roles, goals, and effectiveness of development actions and agreed on several significant points with an agenda.

• The 8 Millennium Development Goals (MDGs)

In 2000, the Millennium Summit adopted the UN Millennium Declaration which contains fundamental values of international relations in the 21st century, central challenges, new global partnership goals and many other issues that the world needs to deal with. The Millennium Development Goals (MDGs) were included in the declaration.

The MDGs are a series of goals that the world agreed to cooperate with each other in order to achieve these goals to achieve by 2015. The goals were primary targets that were thought to be a solution in dealing with the reduction of extreme poverty. It has its significance in that it was the first time the world settled on a direction of global partnership for the international development cooperation in a longer term, especially putting the needs of the developing countries first in the center of their discussion. So after the MDGs were set, they provided a basic structure of activities regarding the development issues in governmental organizations and international organizations.

MDGs consist of 8 goals and 25 targets. Targets are the sub fields of practice within the 8 goals. Originally, there were 21 targets, but in 2007, 4 new targets were included, which were

agreed on by the 2005 World Summit. Several indicators for measuring the achievement of each target were used to examine the progress of the development goals.

The goals and targets of MDGs are as follows:

Goal 1. Eradicate extreme poverty and hunger

1.A	Halve, between 1990 and 2015, the proportion of people whose income is less than one dollar a day
1.B	Achieve full and productive employment and decent work for all, including women and young people
1.C	Halve, between 1990 and 2015, the proportion of people suffer from hunger

Goal 2. Achieve universal primary education

2.A	Ensure that, by 2015, children everywhere, boys and girls alike, will be able to complete a full course of primary schooling

Goal 3. Promote gender equality and empower women

3.A	Eliminate gender disparity in primary and secondary education, preferably by 2005, and in all levels of education no later than 2015

Goal 4. Reduce child mortality

4.A	Reduce by two-thirds, between 1990 and 2015, the under-five mortality rate

Goal 5. Improve maternal health

5.A	Reduce by three quarters, between 1990 and 2015, the maternal mortality ratio
5.B	Achieve, by 2015, universal access to reproductive health

Goal 6. Combat HIV/AIDS, malaria and other diseases

6.A	Have halted by 2015 and begun to reverse the spread of HIV/AIDS
6.B	Achieve, by 2010, universal access to treatment for HIV/AIDS for all those who need it
6.C	Have halted by 2015 and begun to reverse the incidence of malaria and other major diseases

Goal 7. Ensure environmental sustainability

7.A	Integrate the principles of sustainable development into country policies and programmes and reverse the loss of environmental resources
7.B	Reduce biodiversity loss, achieving, by 2010, a significant reduction in the rate of loss
7.C	Halve, by 2015, the proportion of people without sustainable access to safe drinking water and basic sanitation
7.D	By 2020, to have achieved a significant improvement in the lives of at least 100 million slum dwellers

Goal 8. Develop a global partnership for development

8.A	Develop further an open, rule-based, predictable, non-discriminatory trading and financial system
8.B	Address the special needs of the least developed countries

8.C	Address the special needs of landlocked developing countries and small island developing States (through the Programme of Action for the Sustainable Development of Small Island Developing States and the outcome of the twenty-second special session of the General Assembly)
8.D	Deal comprehensively with the debt problems of developing countries through national and international measures in order to make debt sustainable in the long term
8.E	In cooperation with pharmaceutical companies, provide access to affordable essential drugs in developing countries
8.F	In cooperation with the private sector, make available the benefits of new technologies, especially information and communications

MDGs were concluded in domestic policies related to development issues in countries, and development actors in the domestic and global arenas have put much effort to produce positive results. However, there were setbacks mainly caused by financial and economic crises, food security issues and many obstacles that hinder the progress of MDGs. For observation of the difficulties, the leaders attended the UN summit in September, 2010 and reaffirmed the world's commitment to the MDGs. As a result of the summit, a global action plan-*Keeping the Promise: United to Achieve the Millennium Development Goals*- was adopted and several initiatives against poverty, hunger, and disease were announced. Especially, the progress on women's and children's health was seen as the main challenge. The MDG Gap Task Force Report of 2011 of the UN also pointed out that the economic crisis made the commitment to and achievement of MDGs became much harder and even more urgent.

• Paris Declaration and Accra Agenda for Action

The High Level Forum on Aid Effectiveness (HLF) played a big role in deepening and broadening development cooperation and the delivery of aid. The Paris Declaration and Accra Agenda for Action are the outcome of the fora.

Paris Declaration

At the Second High Level Forum on Aid Effectiveness in 2005, it was recognized that aid could and should be producing bigger impacts. The Paris Declaration is an action-oriented roadmap for development cooperation to improve the quality of aid and its impact. It gives a specific monitoring system of progress and, essentially, five principles for aid effectiveness.

- **Ownership**: Developing countries set their own strategies for poverty reduction, improve their institutions and tackle corruption.
- **Alignment**: Donor countries align behind these objectives and use local systems.
- **Harmonization**: Donor countries coordinate, simplify procedures and share information to avoid duplication.
- **Results**: Developing countries and donors shift focus to development results and results get measured.
- **Mutual accountability**: Donors and partners are accountable for development results.

Accra Agenda for Action

The Third High Level Forum on Aid Effectiveness was held in Accra, 2008. A much greater number of stakeholders from different sectors endorsed the Accra Agenda for Action (AAA), which reaffirmed commitment to the Paris Declaration and called for partnership between different parties in the international development cooperation society. The main point of AAA is the part that proposes four main areas for the improvement of the effectiveness.

- **Ownership**: Countries have more say over their development processes through wider participation in development policy formulation, stronger leadership on aid co-ordination and more use of country systems for aid delivery.
- **Inclusive partnerships**: All partners-including donors in the OECD Development Assistance Committee and developing countries, as well as other donors, foundations and civil society-participate fully.
- **Delivering results**: Aid is focused on real and measurable impacts on development.
- **Capacity development**: This also lies at the heart of the AAA to build the ability of countries to manage their own future.

• Busan Partnership Agreement

The Fourth High Level Forum on Aid Effectiveness in Busan, 2011, brought over 3000 delegates together and discussed collective plans for future development and aid. The outcome document, Busan Partnership for Effective Development Cooperation, was signed by delegates from developed and developing countries, from the North and the South, including civil societies. It has significance in that for the first time this declaration established an agreed framework for development cooperation that embraces traditional donors, South-South co-operators, the BRICS, civil society organizations and private funders.

2. New Paradigms for the Development Activities in the International Society

• The Rio+20 Conference

While pushing the progress of MDGs, the world started to prepare the next agenda, Sustainable Development Goals, which would replace MDGs after its deadline in 2015. There were several discussions in international society about the next agenda, and the Rio+20 Conference was the main starting point of the next discourse. The Rio+20 Conference, of which the original name is the United Nations Conference on Sustainable Development, discussed mainly two themes: green economy in the context of sustainable development and poverty eradication and international co-operation for sustainable development. Member States which gathered in the conference decided to launch a process to develop a set of Sustainable Development Goals (SDGs).

• **Post-2015 Development Agenda**

Ope Working Group (OWG) of the General Assembly is tasked with preparing a proposal on the SDGs, following the outcome of the Rio+20 Conference. At the Rio+20, specific goals were not stated, but it stated that SDGs should be limited in number, aspirational and easy to communicate. Also, the goals should address in a balanced way all three dimensions of sustainable development and be coherent with and integrated into the UN development agenda beyond 2015. Through over two years of sessions, consultation and engagement with international development actors including civil society and other stakeholders, the OWG concluded the proposal on Sustainable Development Goals with specific goals and targets. The proposal was discussed at the Sustainable Development Summit in September 2015, and the outcome document, *Transforming our world: the 2030 Agenda for Sustainable Development*, included what the Member States agreed. Below is the preamble of *Transforming our world: the 2030 Agenda for Sustainable Development:*

This Agenda is a plan of action for people, planet and prosperity. It also seeks to strengthen universal peace in larger freedom. We recognize that eradicating poverty in all its forms and dimensions, including extreme poverty, is the greatest global challenge and an indispensable requirement for sustainable development. All countries and all stakeholders, acting in collaborative partnership, will implement this plan. We are resolved to free the human race from the tyranny of poverty and want and to heal and secure our planet. We are determined to take the bold and transformative steps which are urgently needed to shift the world onto a sustainable and resilient path. As we embark on this collective journey, we pledge that no one will be left behind. The 17 Sustainable Development Goals and 169 targets which we are announcing today demonstrate the scale and ambition of this new universal Agenda. They seek to build on the Millennium Development Goals and complete what these did not achieve. They seek to realize the human rights of all and to achieve gender equality and the empowerment of all women and girls. They are integrated and indivisible and balance the three dimensions of sustainable development: the economic, social and environmental.

The Goals and targets will stimulate action over the

next fifteen years in areas of critical importance for humanity and the planet:

People

We are determined to end poverty and hunger, in all their forms and dimensions, and to ensure that all human beings can fulfil their potential in dignity and equality and in a healthy environment.

Planet

We are determined to protect the planet from degradation, including through sustainable consumption and production, sustainably managing its natural resources and taking urgent action on climate change, so that it can support the needs of the present and future generations.

Prosperity

We are determined to ensure that all human beings can enjoy prosperous and fulfilling lives and that economic, social and technological progress occurs in harmony with nature.

Peace

We are determined to foster peaceful, just and inclusive societies which are free from fear and violence. There can be no sustainable development without peace and no peace without sustainable development.

Partnership

We are determined to mobilize the means required to implement this Agenda through a revitalised Global Partnership for Sustainable Development, based on a spirit of strengthened global solidarity, focussed in particular on the needs of the poorest and most vulnerable and with the participation of all countries, all stakeholders and all people.

The interlinkages and integrated nature of the Sustainable Development Goals are of crucial importance in ensuring that the purpose of the new Agenda is realised. If we realize our ambitions across the full extent of the Agenda, the lives of all will be profoundly improved and our world will be transformed for the better.

• Sustainable Development Goals (SDGs)

SDGs were the set of goals built upon MDGs, and the post-2015 development agenda. As a part of it, Member States decided to establish a High-Level Political Forum (HLPF) on Sustainable Development which would subsequently replace the Commission of Sustainable Development. Also, the Conference discussed thematic areas, including energy, food security, and cities which connect to SDGs' discourse. Basically, the Agenda is a plan of action for people, planet and prosperity, and it recognizes that eradication of poverty is required to achieve sustainable development. As the Rio+20 stated, the goals and targets are balanced in the three dimensions of Sustainable Development: economic, social, and environmental. Compared to MDGs, SDGs cover much more topics and give much more specific targets, which were based on the MDGs' results and the outcomes of previous discussions. These are the 17 Goals of SDGs.

Goal 1. No Poverty

- End poverty in all its forms everywhere

Goal 2. Zero Hunger

- End hunger, achieve food security and improved nutrition and promote sustainable agriculture

Goal 3. Good Health and Well-Being

- Ensure healthy lives and promote well-being for all at all ages

Goal 4. Quality Education

- Ensure inclusive and equitable quality education and promote lifelong learning opportunities for all

Goal 5. Gender Equality

- Achieve gender equality and empower all women and girls

Goal 6. Clean Water and Sanitation

- Ensure availability and sustainable management of water and sanitation for all

Goal 7. Affordable and Clean Energy

- Ensure access to affordable, reliable, sustainable and modern energy for all

Goal 8. Decent Work and Economic Growth

- Promote sustained, inclusive and sustainable economic growth, full and productive employment and decent work for all

Goal 9. Industry, Innovation and Infrastructure

- Build resilient infrastructure, promote inclusive and sustainable industrialization and foster innovation

Goal 10. Reduced Inequalities

- Reduce inequality within and among countries

Goal 11. Sustainable Cities and Communities

- Make cities and human settlements inclusive, safe, resilient and sustainable

Goal 12. Responsible Consumption and Production

- Ensure sustainable consumption and production patterns

Goal 13. Climate Action

- Take urgent action to combat climate change and its impacts

Goal 14. Life below Water

- Conserve and sustainably use the oceans, seas and marine resources for sustainable development

Goal 15. Life on Land

- Protect, restore and promote sustainable use of terrestrial ecosystems, sustainably manage forests, combat desertification

Halt and reverse land degradation and halt biodiversity loss

Goal 16. Peace, Justice and Strong Institution

- Promote peaceful and inclusive societies for sustainable development

Provide access to justice for all and build effective, accountable and inclusive institutions at all levels

Goal 17. Partnerships for the Goals

- Strengthen the means of implementation

Revitalize the global partnership for sustainable development

3. Other Systems

• Addis Ababa Action Agenda

Financing is considered the key factor for the success of SDGs. The outcome agreement of the Third International Conference on Financing for Development in July 2015, which is Addis Ababa Action Agenda, provided a strong foundation for implementing a global sustainable development agenda in September 2015 at the Sustainable Development Summit. Also, it provided foundation for countries to finance and adopt SDGs, and to reach an agreement at the UN climate negotiation in Paris in December 2015.

The Addis Ababa Action Agenda helped to forge an enhanced global partnership for universal inclusive economic prosperity and improvement of people's well-being. At the same time, it stated that domestic resource mobilization is central to the agenda. Regarding the issue, countries agreed to measures which aimed at widening the revenue base, improving tax collection, and combating tax evasion. Also, the document contains the importance of aligning private investment with sustainable development, along with the policies and regulatory frameworks.

There was agreement for international co-operation for financing of specific areas where significant investments are needed, such as infrastructure, and other areas to help realize SDGs. Not only that, the document covers cooperation on issues including technology, science, innovation, trade and capacity building. Countries agreed on new initiatives to achieve the goals. To be more specific, Technology Facilitation Mechanism in technology issues, Global Infrastructure Forum for infrastructure issues, and so on.

• Sendai Framework for Disaster Risk Reduction 2015-2030

The Sendai Framework for Disaster Risk Reduction is the outcome document of the Third UN World Conference on Disaster Risk Reduction in Sendai, 2015. It succeeded the Hyogo Framework for Action 2005-2015. It recognizes that the State has the primary role to reduce disaster risk but responsibility should be shared with other stakeholders. It aims "the substantial reduction of disaster risk and losses in lives, livelihoods and health and in the economic, physical, social, cultural and environmental assets of persons, businesses, communities and countries." Assigning the UN Office for Disaster Risk Reduction (UNISDR) the task to support the implementation, follow-up and review of this framework, the document stated 7 global targets, and 4 priorities for action. The 4 priorities are as follows:

- Priority 1. Understanding disaster risk

Disaster risk management should be based on an understanding of disaster risk in all its dimensions of vulnerability, capacity, exposure of persons and assets, hazard characteristics and the environment. Such knowledge can be used for risk assessment, prevention, mitigation, preparedness and response.

- Priority 2. Strengthening disaster risk governance to manage disaster risk

Disaster risk governance at the national, regional and global levels is very important for prevention, mitigation, preparedness, response, recovery, and rehabilitation. It fosters collaboration and partnership.

- Priority 3. Investing in disaster risk reduction for resilience

Public and private investment in disaster risk prevention and reduction through structural and non-structural measures are essential to enhance the economic, social, health and cultural resilience of persons, communities, countries and their assets, as well as the environment.

- Priority 4. Enhancing disaster preparedness for effective response and to "Build Back Better" in recovery, rehabilitation and reconstruction

The growth of disaster risk means there is a need to strengthen disaster preparedness for response, take action in anticipation of events, and ensure capacities are in place for effective response and recovery at all levels. The recovery, rehabilitation and reconstruction phase is a critical opportunity to build back better, including through integrating disaster risk reduction into development measures.

• SAMOA Pathway

Small Island Developing States (SIDS) Accelerated Modalities of Action, so called the SAMOA Pathway, is the outcome of the Third International Conference on Small Island Developing States in 2014. The SAMOA Pathway set out new modalities of action on various issues including economic growth, climate change, sustainable energy, disaster risk reduction, sustainable use of marine resources, and mean of implementing those objectives.

It reaffirms that small island developing states are in a special case for sustainable development for their vulnerabilities, mainly affected by climate change, and world leaders acknowledged the important role of SIDS in the climate change discourse. The SAMOA Pathway also highlights the need of efforts by SIDS to strengthen the resilience of the impacts of climate change and to improve their adaptive capacity, and promotes energy efficiency and sustainable energy systems. Although it seems the document is focused just on SIDS, it contains the urgent need to ensure partnerships at the national, regional and international level.

Lecture 3. Development Issues and Law, UN

1. Development Issues and Law
2. The Bodies in the UN on the Development Issues and the Legal Basis
3. Other Organs in the UN for the Development issues

Development Issues and Law, UN

1. Development Issues and Law

• Social Actions and Rules

Social inter-actions of the parties produce certain issues within a society. It can be called common interest or common concern of the society because issues are from their living environment and their thoughts, and usually each society shares its own environment and thoughts. So, naturally a society shares interests, which leads to the main issues within the society. Since the government is for addressing social issues and dealing with the problems in order to better the society, the government makes policies out of the issues in a society, which become social promises. Policies and social promises are the basis of regulations and rules. They are also reflected by the law system, in the process of aligning the social system. This leads to social actions of the people of the society.

However, since the parties and environment in the international society differ from those of regional societies and national societies, social interaction among the members is different in all stages. This means, following the linkage in the previous paragraph, different law systems exist in each society in different stages.

• Development Issues and Law

Around development issues, the logic from the issues applies the same way to the social actions. Policies and promises of the participants, mainly donors and recipients, are based on the social issues, and those become the basis of regulations and laws. However, as there is the international society and national societies, which stand as different stages, international development law and national development law contain different issues from each other.

• International Law

International law covers a range of issues, for instance, trade, environment, peace and war, food and agriculture, human rights, poverty, aid and etc. By addressing those issues that the parties in the international society concern, international law governs international systems through law itself and through the institutions which manage the related issues. The main sources of international law are as below;

- International Treaties (Conventions or Agreements)
- Resolutions of international organizations
- Custom
- General Principles of Law
- Judicial decisions
- Writings of publicists

As we live in a society where all nations are connected, international laws and national laws interact each other. National laws are influenced by cooperation, negotiation and the practice of international law in the international stage, and reflect the national issues. After collecting and processing opinions in the society, national governments or institutions apply and enforce the international laws within the national stage.

• ODA Actions and Law

Specifically in development issues, because development cooperation is an action between international actors, national law is affected by international law. ODA is governmental action in international society on the development issues. When ODA was introduced, the international polices, economies, and politics were related to the action work in the international stage.

International Development Law is the most relevant international law to the development issues, and it works in relation to the national laws. It applies to states and international organizations on the issues of development, and governmental actions by the states or the organizations.

2. The Bodies in the UN on the Development Issues and the Legal Basis

• The United Nations (UN) and the legal basis

The United Nations, UN, was established in 1945 after the World War II was ovcr. Thc intcrnational organization has 193 Member States, and has main organizations within itself to govern and cooperate with international actors. The General Assembly, the Security Council, the Economic and Social Council and other numerous bodies and committees are under the UN system.

It has its fundamental legal basis in Charter of the United Nations, and the main purpose of the UN is: 1) to keep international peace and security, 2) to develop friendly relations among the members, 3) to help nations work together to improve the lives of poor people, to conquer hunger/disease/illiteracy, to encourage respect for each other's rights and freedoms, and 4) to be a center for harmonizing the actions of nations.

Regarding the development issues, we can look into Chapter IX (Article 55-60), which states international economic and social cooperation issue and the main purposes and directions of the UN, and Chapter X (Article 61-72), which is about the composition and function of the Economic and Social Council (ECOSOC) that works as the main frame in the UN.

• CHAPTER IX of the UN Charter
- International Economic and Social Cooperation

Article 55

With a view to the creation of conditions of stability and well-being which are necessary for peaceful and friendly relations among nations based on respect for the principle of equal rights and self-determination of peoples, the United Nations shall promote:

- higher standards of living, full employment, and conditions of economic and social progress and development;
- solutions of international economic, social, health, and related problems; and international cultural and educational cooperation; and
- universal respect for, and observance of, human rights and fundamental freedoms for all without distinction as to race, sex, language, or religion.

Article 56

All Members pledge themselves to take joint and separate action in co-operation with the Organization for the achievement of the purposes set forth in Article 55.

Article 57

- The various specialized agencies, established by intergovernmental agreement and having wide international responsibilities, as defined in their basic instruments, in economic, social, cultural, educational, health, and related fields, shall be brought into relationship with the United Nations in accordance with the provisions of Article 63.
- Such agencies thus brought into relationship with the United Nations are hereinafter referred to as specialized agencies.

Article 58

The Organization shall make recommendations for the co-ordination of the policies and activities of the specialized agencies.

Article 59

The Organization shall, where appropriate, initiate negotiations among the states concerned for the creation of any new specialized agencies required for the accomplishment of the purposes set forth in Article 55.

Responsibility for the discharge of the functions of the Organization set forth in this Chapter shall be vested in the General Assembly and, under the authority of the General Assembly, in the Economic and Social Council, which shall have for this purpose the powers set forth in Chapter X.

• The Economic and Social Council (ECOSOC)

The Economic and Social Council (ECOSOC) is the principal organ in coordinating economic, social, and related work in the UN system. It is the central forum for discussing international economic and social issues, and for formulating policy recommendations. It functions mainly with 4 purposes: 1) Promoting higher standards of living, full employment, and economic and social progress, 2) Identifying solutions to international economic, social and health problems, 3) Facilitating international cultural and educational cooperation, and 4) Encouraging universal respect for human rights and fundamental freedoms. Organizations for development cooperation, which are well-known in international society, are under the ECOSOC. Chapter X of the UN Charter provides the legal basis on the composition and function of the Economic and Social Council (ECOSOC).

• **CHAPTER X of the UN Charter – ECOSOC**

COMPOSITION

Article 61

- The Economic and Social Council shall consist of fifty-four Memers of the United Nations elected by the General Assembly.
- Subject to the provisions of paragraph 3, eighteen members of the economic and Social Council shall be elected each year for a term of three years. A retiring member shall be eligible for immediate re-election.
- At the first election after the increase in the membership of the Economic and Social Council from twenty-seven to fifty-four members, in addition to the members elected in place of the nine members whose term of office expires at the end of that year, twenty- seven additional members shall be elected. Of these twenty-seven additional members, the term of office of nine members so elected shall expire at the end of one year, and of nine other members at the end of two years, in accordance with arrangements made by the General Assembly.
- Each member of the Economic and Social Council shall have one representative.

FUNCTIONS and POWERS

Article 62

- The Economic and Social Council may make or initiate studies and reports with respect to international economic, social, cultural, educational, health, and related matters and may make recommendations with respect to any such matters to the General Assembly to the Members of the United Nations, and to the specialized agencies concerned.
- It may make recommendations for the purpose of promoting respect for, and observance of, human rights and fundamental freedoms for all.
- It may prepare draft conventions for submission to the General Assembly, with respect to matters falling within its competence.
- It may call, in accordance with the rules prescribed by the United Nations, international conferences on matters falling within its competence.

Article 63

- The Economic and Social Council may enter into agreements with any of the agencies referred to in Article 57, defining the terms on which the agency concerned shall be brought into relationship with the United Nations. Such agreements shall be subject to approval by the General Assembly.

- It may co-ordinate the activities of the specialized agencies through consultation with the recommendations to such agencies and through recommendations to the General Assembly and to the Members of the United Nations.

Article 64

- The Economic and Social Council may take appropriate steps to obtain regular reports from the specialized agencies. It may make arrangements with the Members of the United Nations and with the specialized agencies to obtain reports on the steps taken to give effect to its own recommendations and to recommendations no matters falling within its competence made by the General Assembly.
- It may communicate its observations on these reports to the General Assembly.

Article 65

- The Economic and Social Council may furnish information to the Security Council and shall assist the Security Council upon its request.

Article 66

- The Economic and Social Council shall perform such functions as fall within its competence in connection with the carrying out of the recommendations of the General Assembly.

- It may, with the approval of the General Assembly, perform services at the request of Members of the United Nations and at the request of specialized agencies.
- It shall perform such other functions as are specified elsewhere in the present Charter or as may be assigned to it by the General Assembly.

VOTING

Article 67

- Each member of the Economic and Social Council shall have one vote.
- Decisions of the Economic and Social Council shall be made by a majority of the members present and voting.

PROCEDURE

Article 68

- The Economic and Social Council shall set up commissions in economic and social fields and for the promotion of human rights, and such other commissions as may be required for the performance of its functions.

Article 69

- The Economic and Social Council shall invite any

Member of the United nations to participate, without vote, in its deliberations on any matter of particular concern to that Member.

Article 70

- The Economic and Social Council may make arrangements for representatives of the specialized agencies to participate without vote, in its deliberations and in those of the commissions established by it, and for its representatives to participate in the deliberations of the specialized agencies.

Article 71

- The Economic and Social Council may make suitable arrangements for consultation with non-governmental organizations which are concerned with matters within its competence. Such arrangements may be made with international organizations and, where appropriate, with national organizations after consultation with the Member of the United Nations concerned.

Article 72

- The Economic and Social Council shall adopt its own rules of procedure, including the method of selecting its President.

- The Economic and Social Council shall meet as required in accordance with its rules, which shall include provision for the convening of meetings on the request of a majority of its members.

3. Other Organs in the UN for the Development Issues

• The United Nations Development Programme (UNDP)

The United Nations Development Programme (UNDP) is the global development network under ECOSOC. The UNDP works for eradication of global poverty, and it is the main organization that is in charge of MDGs and SDGs. It can be said that the UNDP covers most of the development issues including environment, energy, health, women's empowerment, and capacity development.

The UN Chapter X is the indirect legal basis of the UNDP in that it states the composition and function of ECOSOC. However, the direct legal basis is the resolution 2029 (XX) and 2688(XXV) of the General Assembly. The resolution 2029 (XX) is about the consolidation of the Special Fund (UNSF) and the Expanded Programme of Technical Assistance (UNEPTA) in the UNDP, and the resolution 2688(XXV) is about the organization and operation of UNDP.

• The United Nations Educational, Scientific and Cultural Organization (UNESCO)

The United Nations Educational, Scientific and Cultural Organization (UNESCO) is a specialized agency which contributes to the building of peace, development, and intercultural dialogue through education, science, culture, communication and information. It puts priority on Africa and gender equality. Under its mission, the main objectives of UNESCO are as follows:

- Attaining quality education for all and lifelong learning
- Mobilizing science knowledge and policy for sustainable development
- Addressing emerging social and ethical challenges
- Fostering cultural diversity, intercultural dialogue and a culture of peace
- Building inclusive knowledge societies through information and communication

• The United Nations Conference on Trade and Development (UNCTAD)

The United Nations Conference on Trade and Development (UNCTAD) main focus is to promote the development-friendly integration of less-developed countries into the world economy. The UNCTAD focuses on ensuring that two stages, the national stage and the international stage, are inter-supportive regarding sustainable development issues. In development fields, the UNCTAD functions as the forum for intergovernmental deliberations, institution for research and policy analysis, and as a provider of technical assistance tailored to the specific requirements of less-developed countries.

Lecture 4.
ODA and Trade Issues, WTO

1. Development Issues and Aid for Trade

2. The World Trade Organization (WTO)

3. The SDGs in the WTO

4. The Law for the Works

ODA and Trade Issues, WTO

1. Development Issues and Aid for Trade

• Concept of Aid for Trade

Economic growth may alleviate poverty of developing countries, helping them to reach their development goals. Trade can promote the economic growth of countries. However, developing countries (in particular the LDC/least developed countries) may have many practical difficulties in making their own trade and turning trade into economic growth. Therefore, the international society is supporting developing countries to foster economic growth and reduce poverty under the concept of Aid for Trade.

The Concept of Aid for Trade is to help unlock the potential of developing countries to benefit from trade, fostering a transparent and mutually beneficial relationship between developing countries and donors. The WTO defines the concept of *Aid for*

Trade as below;

> *"Aid for trade is about assisting developing countries to increase exports of goods and services, to integrate into the multilateral trading system, and to benefit from liberalised trade and increased market access."*
> (The WTO Task Force on Aid for Trade [WT/AFT/1], 27 July 2006)

The concept of Aid for Trade is close to the positive relationship between trade and growth, considering the focus on opening up the domestic economy to foreign trade, investment and competition, and integration into the world trading system. This activity is based on the opinion "some indicator of external openness is strongly associated with per capita income growth". Many researchers have proved that there is no country that has grown successfully without a large expansion of its trade. Also, some reports of Least Developed Country (LDC) show that the proportion of people living on less than one dollar a day appears to increase significantly and relatively to the degree of export variety in LDCs.

Aid for Trade is not a new global development fund, nor a new aid category. It is an integral part of regular ODA programmes of developed countries and one of the main subjects in the UR aiming at technical support to help developing countries. Aid for Trade is about helping developing countries, in particular the least developed, to build the trade capacity and infrastructure they need to benefit from opening trade. It is part of overall Official Development Assistance (ODA) — grants and concessional loans — targeted at trade-related programmes and projects.

Aid for Trade (AfT) was endorsed at the WTO's Hong Kong Ministerial Conference in 2005. Since then, Aid for Trade has been considered as a new promising development tool for helping developing countries benefit under WTO agreements and expanding their trade. Thus, the definition of AfT has been broadened to include trade-related infrastructures, building productive capacity and trade-related adjustment. Since there are challenges of widening the definition of AfT (For example, definitions different among donor countries or international organizations, and lack of financial contributions), AfT should enhance its monitoring system and be careful.

Adjusting AfT systems into transparent management systems will let developing countries and developed countries both benefit. Since fixing its system and maintaining it reduces the costs of trade and increase its productivity. Therefore, effective monitoring and evaluation is needed. Although WTO is not a development agency and should not become one, (its role is trade opening and dispute settlement), WTO does have a role and responsibility to ensure that members of WTO work together more effectively. WTO provides three monitoring levels: 'Global level', 'Donor level', and 'Country and regional level'. It aims at the "spotlight effect", which provides incentives when there is progress so that the demand side, supply side, private sector will all be foster synergies.

• The Main Methods and Categories

The projects and programmes of AfT should be identified as trade-related development priorities. Therefore, the WTO and OECD joint database follows categories that the WTO task force provides while planning and monitoring programmes.

– Technical assistance for trade policy and regulations:

Helping countries to develop trade strategies, negotiate trade agreements, and implement their outcomes.

– Trade-related infrastructure:

Building roads, ports, and telecommunications networks to connect domestic markets to the global economy.

– Productive capacity building, including trade development:

Supporting the private sector to exploit their comparative advantages and diversify their exports.

– Trade-related adjustment:

Helping developing countries with the costs associated with trade liberalisation, such as tariff reductions, preference erosion, or declining terms of trade.

2. The World Trade Organization (WTO)

• WTO

The WTO is an organization for liberalizing trade. It's a forum for governments to negotiate trade agreements. It's a place for them to settle trade disputes. It operates a system of trade rules. The WTO began life on 1 January 1995, but its trading system is half a century older. Since 1948, the General Agreement on Tariffs and Trade (GATT) had provided the rules for the system. The last and largest GATT round, was the Uruguay Round which lasted from 1986 to 1994 and led to the WTO's creation. Whereas GATT had mainly dealt with trade in goods, the WTO and its agreements now cover trade in services, and in traded inventions, creations and designs (intellectual property).

• Role of the WTO for "Aid for Trade"

The role of the WTO in the field of AfT is to mobilize, monitor and evaluate AfT. The WTO encourages additional flows of Aid for Trade from bilateral, regional and multilateral donors to support requests for trade-related capacity-building from beneficiary countries. Furthermore, the WTO and the OECD have jointly developed a monitoring and evaluation framework that helps create incentives through better transparency, etc.

• The Bodies on the Development Issues in the WTO System

The WTO system includes Committee on Trade and Development and its Sub-Committee on Least-Developed Countries. The Committee on Trade and Development is mandated to provide guidelines for the **technical assistance** activities of the WTO and to review, periodically, these activities. Technical Assistance is so called TRTA (**Trade-Related Technical Assistance**). **Technical assistance** and training are core elements of the development dimension so as to enhance the human and institutional capacities of beneficiaries to take full advantage of the rule-based Multilateral Trading System.

The WTO Agreements contain special provisions which give developing countries special rights and which give developed countries the possibility to treat developing countries more favourably than other WTO Members. These special provisions include, for example, longer time periods for implementing Agreements and commitments or measures to increase trading opportunities for developing countries. These provisions are referred to as "**special and differential treatment**" (S&D) provisions. The Ministers in Doha, at the 4th WTO Ministerial Conference mandated the Committee on Trade and Development to examine these special and differential treatment provisions. The special provisions include:

- Longer time periods for implementing Agreements and

commitments,

- Measures to increase trading opportunities for developing countries,
- Provisions requiring all WTO members to safeguard the trade interests of developing countries,
- Support to help developing countries build the capacity to carry out WTO work, handle disputes, and implement technical standards, and
- Provisions related to least-developed country (LDC) Members.

Small economies face specific challenges in participating in world trade due to lack of economy of scale or limited natural resources, for example. The Doha Declaration mandates the General Council to make recommendations as to what trade-related measures could improve the integration of **small economies** into the multilateral trading system, without creating a separate category of WTO members.

The WTO has been working for LDCs. LDCs are the countries that UN designated. There are currently 48 least-developed countries on the UN list, 34 of which to date have become WTO members. Developing LDCs is closely related to trade, since those countries are countries that are least-developed under the circumstance of un-openness in trade area. Following countries are LDCs designated by UN:

Angola/Bangladesh/Benin/Burkina Faso/Burundi/Cambodia/Central African Republic/Chad/ Congo, Democratic Republic of the/Djibouti/Gambia/Guinea/Guinea Bissau/Haiti/ Lao People's Democratic Republic/Lesotho/Madagascar Malawi/Mali/Mauritania/Mozambique/Myanmar Nepal Niger/ Rwanda/Senegal/Sierra Leone/Solomon Islands/Tanzania/Togo Uganda/Vanuatu/Yemen/Zambia

• MDGs and WTO

The work of the WTO is relevant to achieving a number of the MDGs, but specifically the organization's core activities fall mainly within the objectives of MDG 8, a global partnership for development. MDG 8 is therefore an important element in the overall structure of the MDGs. While all MDGs are important in helping countries reach a level of development conducive to the elimination of extreme poverty, MDG 8 is the precondition for all of these goals to be sustainable in the long run.

MDG 8, which is WTO's mostly involved sector, is also aiming 6 targets. The six targets identified under MDG 8 show that the international community recognizes that open trade is an important engine for development. **Target A** is a target that aims for Developing further an open, rule-based, predictable, non-discriminatory trading and financial system. For trade to deliver real economic growth effectively, it needs to be "open, rule-based, predictable and non-discriminatory", as recognized in **Target A**. This corresponds to the WTO's core business of regulating international trade, reducing market barriers and ensuring a level playing field for all its members. **Target B** is aiming for addressing the special needs of the LDCs. The WTO is also committed to working towards enhancing the benefits that can accrue to the poorest of its members. In designing its rules, the WTO recognizes the capacity constraints of these countries in taking on trade-related commitments. **Target C** addresses the special needs of landlocked developing countries and small island developing states. **Target D** aims to deal comprehensively with the debt problems of developing countries. **Target E**, in cooperation with pharmaceutical companies, provides access to affordable essential drugs in developing countries. **Target F**, in cooperation with the private sector, makes available the benefits of new technologies, especially information and communication. This is partly addressed by WTO work in increasing flows of technology to developing countries. By identifying technology and innovation as critical drivers of economic growth, the WTO has indicated that technology innovation and its transfer are important for the achievement of the MDGs.

• DDA Round

At the Fourth Ministerial Conference in Doha, Qatar, in November 2001, WTO members agreed to launch new negotiation which is called the Doha Development Agenda Round dealing with multinational trade negotiation. DDA has a meaningful history in the fact that it is the latest negotiation that discusses new issues on trade and development. The majority of WTO Members are developing countries. This DDA, therefore, has the purpose of ensuring that developing countries are provided with the trade opportunities that will enhance their growth and development prospects.

A fundamental aspect of the Doha Round of negotiations is that it addresses some of the imbalances in trade rules that have disadvantages towards developing country exports. This is to ensure that the rules under consideration provide developing countries with real market opportunities and, accordingly, opportunities to enhance their development and growth prospects. The development dimension can be adopted in all negotiating areas. When the Doha Round is concluded, the multilateral trading system will be more open and will have a strengthened rule-making structure that will be more balanced, especially towards developing country interests and concerns. There is, therefore, a clear connection between concluding the DDA negotiations and bringing about MDG 8. A successful conclusion of the Doha Round would, thus, go a long way in addressing developing country needs and contribute significantly to the achievement of MDG 8.

3. The SDGs in the WTO

• SDGs in the WTO System : new paradigm for the WTO works

The SDGs put significant emphasis on the role that trade can play in promoting sustainable development. There are direct references to WTO activities in many of the SDGs. Among 17 SDGs that were mentioned in advance, the WTO activities are heading towards the same direction as **SDG 2** (Zero Hunger) on hunger, food security, nutrition and sustainable agriculture, **SDG 3** (Good Health and Well-Being) on healthy lives and wellbeing, **SDG 8** (Decent Work and Economic Growth) on economic growth, employment and work, **SDG 10** (Reduced Inequalities) on inequalities within and among countries, **SDG 14** (Life below Water) on oceans, seas, and marine resources, **SDG 17** (Partnerships for the Goals) on strengthening the global partnership for sustainable development contains a separate section on trade. Each goal of 'sustainable development' has several different targets related to trade, which is WTO works, and therefore WTO is accepting the new paradigm that SDGs have provided.

The WTO is focusing on mainly 5 big trade related SDGs issues. **'Trade to promote growth and reduce poverty', 'Trade as a long-term strategy against hunger', 'Trade and Environment', 'Flexibility', 'Trade for the energy technologies'** are categories of those issues. Following descriptions are how those topics match with WTO works and what the legal bases of their operation are.

• Trade to promote growth and reduce poverty

The SDGs' main theme is the integration of developing countries into regional and global markets. To help achieve this objectives, the SDGs seek to ensure that trade plays its part in boosting growth, tackling poverty and promoting sustainable development. Thus, relating to trade, SDGs have a clear identification in priority on the following statement:

Firstly, SDG 8 (Decent Work and Economic Growth) intends to increase AfT support for developing countries, in particular the least-developed countries (LDCs). Based on the provision of Target 8 (a), WTO's work should be involved in promoting Aid for Trade assisting LDCs.

> SDG 8. Target (a)
> Increase Aid for Trade support for developing countries, in particular least developed countries, including through the Enhanced Integrated Framework for Trade-related Technical Assistance to Least Developed Countries.

Secondly, SDG 10(Reduced Inequalities) is about the principle of "special and different treatment" for LDCs to be implemented.. So far, achieving SDG 10 has its evidence on target (a). Target

(a) guarantees LDCs the 'special and different treatment' while trading.

SDG 10. Target (a)
Implement the principle of special and differential treatment for developing countries, in particular least developed countries, in accordance with World Trade Organization agreements.

Thirdly, According to Target 11 of SDG 17(Partnerships for the Goals), the WTO put efforts into increasing the exports of developing countries, in particular with a view on doubling the LDCs' share of global exports by 2020. Also, Target 12 of SDG 17(Partnerships for the Goals) is providing an implementation of duty-free and quota-free market access on a lasting basis for all LDCs, ensuring that preferential rules of origin applicable to imports from LDCs are transparent and simple, and contribute to facilitating market access.

SDG 17. Target 10
Promote a universal, rules-based, open, non-discriminatory and equitable multilateral trading system under the World Trade Organization, including through the conclusion of negotiations under its Doha Development Agenda.

SDG 17. Target 11

Significantly increase the exports of developing countries, in particular with a view to doubling the least developed countries' share of global exports by 2020.

SDG 17. Target 12

Realise timely implementation of duty-free and quota-free market access on a lasting basis for all least developed countries, consistent with World Trade Organization decisions, including by ensuring that preferential rules of origin applicable to imports from least developed countries are transparent and simple, and contribute to facilitating market access.

• Trade as a long-term strategy against hunger

The SDGs recognize that a more open, transparent and well-functioning global agricultural market is an essential element of a wider strategy to end hunger, achieve food security and improved nutrition, and promote sustainable agriculture. However, Policies that distort production and trade in agricultural commodities can undermine efforts to realize these goals, because they often stimulate inefficient and costly production where it would not otherwise occur and prevent the most competitive producers, many of which are located in developing countries, from participating in global trade. Therefore, the WTO is taking on its work by following Target (b) of SDG 2 (zero hunger) which calls for an end to trade restrictions and distortions in world agricultural markets.

> SDG 2. Target (b)
>
> Correct and prevent trade restrictions and distortions in world agricultural markets, including through the parallel elimination of all forms of agricultural export subsidies and all export measures with equivalent effect, in accordance with the mandate of the Doha Development Round.

- **Trade and Environment** **(A win-win for trade and the environment)**

The conservation and sustainable use of the oceans, seas and marine resources is an essential element in promoting sustainable development. Amid growing concerns about the problems of overcapacity and overfishing in today's modern fishery fleets, and the role that subsidization could play in exacerbating these problems, Target 6 of SDG 14(Life below Water) calls for a prohibition by 2020 on certain forms of fishery subsidiaries that contribute to overcapacity and overfishing, and to eliminate subsidies that contribute to illegal, unreported and unregulated fishing. The WTO is not only following rules that Target 6 provides, but also keeps small island developing states and the least developed countries protected in using marine resources. This is the very agenda of SAMOA Pathway which is already discussed in Chapter 2.

> SDG 14. Target 6
>
> By 2020, prohibit certain forms of fisheries subsidies which contribute to overcapacity and overfishing, eliminate subsidies that contribute to illegal, unreported and unregulated fishing and refrain from introducing new such subsidies, recognizing that appropriate and effective special and differential treatment for developing and least developed countries should be an integral part of the World Trade Organization fisheries subsidies negotiation 16.

> SDG 14. Target 7
>
> By 2030, increase the economic benefits to small island developing States and least developed countries from the sustainable use of marine resources, including through sustainable management of fisheries, aquaculture and tourism.

• Flexibilities to protect public health

SDG(Good health and well-being) on ensuring healthy lives and promoting wellbeing, includes the target of providing "access to affordable essential medicines and vaccines". It recalls the

2001 Doha Declaration on the TRIPS Agreement and Public Health, which affirms the right to use to the full the provisions in the TRIPS Agreement regarding flexibilities to protect public health, and, in particular, provide access to medicines for all. So far, many works of the WTO are related to SDG 3 and the WTO put efforts to be assessed as good by following Target (b).

> SDG 3. Target (b)
> Support the research and development of vaccines and medicines for the communicable and non-communicable diseases that primarily affect developing countries, provide access to affordable essential medicines and vaccines, in accordance with the Doha Declaration on the TRIPS Agreement and Public Health, which affirms the right of developing countries to use to the full the provisions in the Agreement on Trade-Related Aspects of Intellectual Property Rights regarding flexibilities to protect public health, and, in particular, provide access to medicines for all.

• Trade for the energy technologies

SDG 7(Affordable and clean energy) does not directly mention trade but it underlines the importance of "international cooperation to facilitate access to clean energy research and technology, including renewable energy, energy efficiency and advanced and cleaner fossil-fuel technology". WTO's work is still mandating aim on Target (a). Among the myriad expressions of cooperation in the field of technology is the elimination of barriers that hinders the movement of green goods and services between countries. More open trade in such goods and services should make them cheaper and more accessible to producers and consumers around the world, lowering the cost of attaining key environmental protection goals in developing and developed countries alike.

> SDG 7. Target (a)
>
> By 2030, enhance international cooperation to facilitate access to clean energy research and technology, including renewable energy, energy efficiency and advanced and cleaner fossil-fuel technology, and promote investment in energy infrastructure and clean energy technology.

4. The Law for the Works

• The Special And Different Provisions in the WTO Agreements

Unlike former conventions that generated WTO, the GATT, UR, DDA are not counted within the same category of WTO treatments. DDA has a name of 'Development Agenda' which is specifically different from 'Round'. After UR, participation of developing countries in the WTO has been increasing rapidly. UR has been enhancing mandates by including areas that GATT couldn't cover. However, developing countries are arguing that this single-undertaking principle of UR is oppressing them to follow helpless orders such as TRIPS. Therefore, developing countries start to insist that the WTO should not aim on only expanding free trade but aim on economic development of the whole world by using trade. Supporting those ideas of developing countries, bureau-meeting in Doha agreed to name itself a 'Development Agenda' rather than a 'Round'.

The WTO Agreements contain special provisions which give developing countries special rights and which give developed countries the possibility to treat developing countries more favourably than the other WTO Members. These special provisions include, for example, longer time periods for implementing Agreements and commitments or measures to increase trading opportunities for developing countries. These provisions are referred to as "special and differential treatment" (S and D) provisions.

The special provisions include longer time periods for implementing Agreements and commitments, measures to increase trading opportunities for developing countries, provisions requiring all WTO members to safeguard the trade interests of developing countries, support to help developing countries build the capacity to carry out WTO work, handle disputes, and implement technical standards, and provisions related to least-developed country (LDC) Members.

The agreement establishing the WTO, GATT, GATS, TRIPS includes povisions that support LDCs' trade. The agreement establishing the WTO is promoting that sustainable economic development shall be one of the objectives of the WTO. Also, this agreement specifies that international trade should benefit the economic development of developing and least-developed countries. The following statement is an introduction of AGREEMENT ESTABLISHING THE WORLD TRADE ORGANIZATION that mandating protecting LDCs right on trade.

> *"Recognizing further that there is need for positive efforts designed to ensure that developing countries, and especially the least developed among them, secure a share in the growth in international trade commensurate with the needs of their economic development,"*

• GATT 1994

Basically, 'Special and Different Treatment' issues have been raised for a half century after GATT. For instance, GATT's Article XVIII is allowing developing countries to build safeguard action for Balance of payments. Especially after 1955, the amendment has added Section B in Article XVIII which provides easier conditions for developing countries than developed one.

GATT Article XVIII, to be read in conjunction with the Decision on Safeguard action for Development Purposes and the Declaration on Trade Measures Taken for Balance-of-payments Purposes, both of 28 November 1979, and the Understanding on the Balance-of Payments Provisions of the GATT 1994, gives developing countries the right to restrict imports, if doing so would promote the establishment or maintenance of a particular industry, or assist in cases of balance-of-payments difficulties. Part IV of the GATT includes provisions on the concept of non-reciprocal preferential treatment for developing countries — when developed countries grant trade concessions to developing countries they should not expect the developing countries to make matching offers in return. Nonreciprocal preferential treatment refers to a trade arrangement under which one party agrees to extend preferential treatment to the imports of a country or group of countries unilaterally.

> Article XXXVI 1.
>
> The contracting parties, (f) noting that the CONTRACTING PARTIES may enable less-developed contracting parties to use special measures to promote their trade and development;"
>
> Section Bb.
>
> **8.** The contracting parties recognize that contracting parties coming within the scope of paragraph 4(a) of

this Article tend, when they are in rapid process of development, to experience balance-of-payments difficulties arising mainly from efforts to expand their internal markets as well as from the instability in their terms of trade.

Article XVIII.

Section B was invoked more than 20 times before the WTO Agreement entered into force. Since then, 14 developing countries have made use of Article XVIII:B.

• GATS

Since the existing system under GATT was only promoting trade in goods, the WTO started to expand its area to service toward 'services' and 'intellectual property.' GATS (General Agreement on Trade in Services) is the very principle of the WTO that promotes trade of services.

While services currently account for over 60 percent of global production and employment, they represent no more than 20 per cent of total trade. This share should not be underestimated, however. Many services, which have long been considered genuine domestic activities, have increasingly become internationally mobile. This trend is likely to continue, owing to the introduction of new transmission technologies (e.g. electronic banking, tele-health or tele-education services), the opening up in many countries of long-entrenched monopolies (e.g. voice telephony and postal services), and regulatory reforms in hitherto tightly regulated sectors such as transport. Combined with changing consumer preferences, such technical and regulatory innovations have enhanced the "tradability" of services and thus, created a need for multilateral disciplines.

The GATS (General Agreement on Trade in Services), however, is also focused on increasing the participation of developing countries in world trade. **Article IV** is the very evidence of these works as shown below;

- The increasing participation of developing country Members in world trade shall be facilitated through negotiated specific commitments, by different Members pursuant to Parts III and IV of this Agreement, relating to:
  · the strengthening of their domestic services capacity and its efficiency and competitiveness, inter alia through access to technology on a commercial basis;
  · the improvement of their access to distribution channels and information networks; and
  · the liberalization of market access in sectors and modes of supply of export interest to them.
- Developed country Members, and to the extent possible other Members, shall establish contact points within two years from the date of entry into force of

the WTO Agreement to facilitate the access of developing country Members' service suppliers to information, related to their respective markets, concerning:

- commercial and technical aspects of the supply of services;
- registration, recognition and obtaining of professional qualifications; and
- the availability of services technology.

The key ideas of the **Article IV** are that GATS let developing countries be better off while trading services with developed countries. Furthermore, it refers, among other things, to strengthening the domestic services competitiveness of developing countries through access to technology and improving their access to information networks. **Article XII** allows developing countries and countries in transition to restrict trade in services for reasons of balance-of-payment difficulties.

Article XII:1

"…It is recognized that particular pressures on the balance of payments of a Member in the process of economic development or economic transition may necessitate the use of restrictions to ensures, inter alia, the maintenance of a level of financial reserves adequate for the implementation of its programme of economic development or economic transition."

• TRIPS

As mentioned, the WTO started to expand its trade area form goods to services and intellectual properties. So far, the Agreement on Trade-Related Aspects of Intellectual Property Rights (TRIPS) is an agreement that rules world trade as a principle of 'Intellectual property rights'. TRIPS was negotiated in the 1986-94 Uruguay Round and introduced intellectual property rules into the multilateral trading system for the first time.

Ideas and knowledge are an increasingly important part of trade. Most of the value of new medicines and other high technology products lies in the amount of invention, innovation, research, design and testing involved. Many products that used to be traded as low-technology goods or commodities now contain a higher proportion of invention and design in their value. Creators can be given the right to prevent others from using their inventions, designs or other creations. These are "intellectual property rights". The Uruguay Round achieved that. The WTO' s TRIPS Agreement is an attempt to narrow the gaps in the way these rights are protected around the world, and to bring them under common international rules. It establishes minimum levels of protection that each government has to give to the intellectual property of fellow WTO members. In doing so, it strikes a balance between the long term benefits and possible short term costs to society.

LDCs are given an extended transition period to protect intellectual property under the TRIPS **Article 66**. This is in recognition of their special requirements, their economic, financial and administrative constraints, and the need for flexibility so that they can create a viable technological base.

Article 66.1c

In view of the special needs and requirements of least-developed country Members, their economic, financial and administrative constraints, and their need for flexibility to create a viable technological base, such Members shall not be required to apply the provisions of this Agreement, other than Articles 3, 4 and 5, for a period of 10 years from the date of application as defined under Article 65.1. The Council for TRIPS shall, upon duly motivated request by a least-developed country Member, accord extensions of this period.

Article 66.2b

Developed country Members shall provide incentives to enterprises and institutions in their territories for the purpose of promoting and encouraging technology transfer to least developed country Members in order to enable them to create a sound and viable technological base.

Article 67b

In order to facilitate the implementation of this Agree-

> ment, developed country Members shall provide, on request and on mutually agreed terms and conditions, technical and financial cooperation in favour of developing and least-developed country Members. Such cooperation shall include assistance in the preparation of laws and regulations on the protection and enforcement of intellectual property rights as well as on the prevention of their abuse, and shall include support regarding the establishment or reinforcement of domestic offices and agencies relevant to these matters, including the training of personnel.

To sum up of all the provisions and agreements, in the Doha Declaration, member governments agreed that all special and differential treatment provisions are an integral part of the WTO agreements, and that these provisions should be reviewed with a view on strengthening them and making them more effective and operational. More specifically, the declaration (together with the Decision on Implementation-Related Issues and Concerns) mandates the Committee on Trade and Development (CTD) to identify which of those special and differential treatment provisions are mandatory, and to consider the legal and practical implications of making mandatory those which are currently non-binding. In addition, the Committee is to consider ways in which developing countries, particularly the LDCs, may be assisted to make best use of special and differential treatment.

Lecture 5.
The Laws on the ODA Works of the OECD

1. The OECD

2. The Laws on the ODA Works

3. DAC in the OECD

4. The Development and ODA Issues In The OECD/DAC

The Laws on the ODA Works of the OECD

1. The OECD

• The history of the OECD

In 1961, in Paris, 18 European countries and the U.S, Canada launched the OECD, which stands for the Organization for Economic Cooperation and Development, in order to promote policies on the economic and social well-being of people around the world. The OECD has its origin on OEEC (Originated from the organization for European Economic Cooperation) and has relations with several other international organizations such as The International Labor organization, Food and Agriculture Organization, International Monetary Fund, World Bank, International Atomic Energy Agency, and many other United Nations bodies.

The OECD defines itself as a forum of countries committed to democracy and the market economy, providing a setting to compare policy experiences, seek answers to common problems, identify good practices, and co-ordinate domestic and international policies. The OECD promotes policies that will improve the economic and social well-being of people around the world. The OECD provides a forum in which governments can work together to share experiences and seek solutions to common problems and measure productivity and global flows of trade and investment. The common thread of OECD's work is a shared commitment to market economies backed by democratic institutions and focused on the wellbeing of all citizens.

The following points are the OECD's core value;

- **Objective**: With the independent and evidence-based analyses and recommendations
- **Open**: With the common understandings of critical global issues
- **Bold**: With the challenging conventional wisdom
- **Pioneering**: With the emerging and long term challenges.
- **Ethical**: With the trust, integrity and transparency

Recently about 34 OECD states are the official members of the OECD.

Australia/Austria/Belgium/Canada/Chile/Czech Republic/Denmark/Estonia/Finland/France/Germany/Greece/Hungary/Iceland/Ireland/Israel/Italy/Japan/

Korea/Luxembourg/Mexico/Netherlands/New Zealand/Norway/Poland/Portugal/Slovak Republic/Slovenia/Spain/Sweden/Switzerland/Turkey/United Kingdom/United States

• The legal basis of the OECD

The OECD has its basis on its convention providing the fundamental (international) law for the establishment of the organization. The Convention includes 21 articles with Preamble explaining the background of the establishment of OECD as succeeding the OEEC. The Convention also provides what the vision of the OECD is. In detail, except the first article of the convention, other articles are mandating other rules related to management of the organization. Under this international law, the OECD has the legal capacity to make official relations with other institutions or countries. Furthermore, it and its staff may enjoy several types of privileges in the international society.

2. The Laws on the ODA Works

• Aims and works

Article 1 of the Convention provides the main aims of the organization. That is, the OECD promotes their policies a) to achieve the highest sustainable economic growth and employment and a rising standard of living in Member countries, while maintaining financial stability, and thus to contribute to the development of the world economy b) to contribute to sound economic expansion in member as well as non-member countries in the process of economic development and c) to contribute to the expansion of world trade on a multilateral, non-discriminatory basis in accordance with international obligations.

Article 2 provides the works or undertakings of the OECD. In the pursuit of the goals, the members will, both individually and jointly, a) promote the efficient use of their economic resources, b) in the scientific and technological field, promote the development of their resources, encourage research and promote vocational training, c) pursue policies designed to achieve economic growth and internal and external financial stability and to avoid developments which might endanger their economies or those of other countries, d) pursue their efforts to reduce or abolish obstacles to the exchange of goods and services and current payments and maintain and extend the liberalization of capital movements, and e) contribute to the economic development of both member and non-member countries in the process of economic development by appropriate means and, in particular, by the flow of capital to those countries, having regard to the importance to their economies of receiving technical assistance and of securing expanding export markets.

- **Construction of the internal and external system**

The structure of the OECD institution is based on the several articles of the Convention. Article 7 and 8 provide issues of the composition and status of the Council. Then, Article 9 and 10 are on the Executive Committee and subsidiary bodies such as the Secretary-General. The Secretary-General shall appoint other staff with the approval of the Council. Article 12 is on the External Relations with non-member states or other institutions. According to the provision, the Organization may establish and maintain relations with non-member states or organizations. Then, they can invite non-member Governments or organizations to participate in activities of the organization.

3. DAC in the OECD

- **DAC : The executive committee on the ODA works of the OECD**

Before OECD launched, there was a DAG (Development Assistance Group) which implemented operations of ODA, which is now changed into Development Assistance Committee (DAC) as it became inside institution for the ODA works in the OECD system. It is a unique forum for sharing views and exchanging lessons. Based on neutrality and high-quality work, DAC is defining and monitoring global standards in key areas of the ODA. Currently, DAC is maintaining participation of about 30 members and observers (The World Bank, IMF and UNDP). Furthermore, the committee is recently opened the doors to talk with non-DAC or OECD member donors (such as China, India, Brazil, Indonesia and South Africa). Recently, the DAC/OECD has 29 members listed below;

> Australia/European Union/Ireland/Norway Spain/Austria Finland/Italy/Poland/Sweden/Belgium/France/Japan/Portugal/Switzerland/Canada/Germany/Luxembourg/Slovakia/United Kingdom/Czech Republic/Greece/Netherlands/Slovenia/United States/South Korea

• DCD and DAC

On official development assistance (ODA), the OECD acts as a watchdog, monitoring aid figures and urging donor countries to live up to their commitments. The DAC, supported by the Development Cooperation Directorate, monitors the development assistance performances of its members through peer reviews in which all members are able to comment on each other's policies. DCD supplies technical expertise for the OECD DAC and helps build consensus among its members and the wider development community to improve development effectiveness.

DCD contributes to developing better policies for better lives by understanding development finance: DCD monitor and share statistics as well as information on the architecture of official development assistance (ODA) and other flows of development finance to help ensure transparency and effectiveness, DCD evaluate development programmes for aid effectiveness and conduct peer reviews in development co-operation to sharpen processes and management.

In order to improve development policies, DCD draw on knowledge and experience across the world and advise on diverse development policy issues including aid for trade, conflict and fragility, environment, gender equality, governance and poverty reduction. These policy issues will be introduced later again. In terms of building partnerships for development, DCD are forming wide-ranging partnerships to leverage collective know-how and facilitate innovative and integrated approaches to development. The DAC supports the UN in ensuring the success of the Sustainable Development Goals and has played a role in forging major international development commitments, including the MDGs and SDGs.

• The law for the DAC : Resolution of the DAC mandate

The DAC works also have their own legal bases with the OECD Convention. According to 'RESOLUTION OF THE COUNCIL REVISING THE MANDATE OF THE DEVELOP-

MENT ASSISTANCE COMMITTEE, 14 December 1960', the overarching objective of the DAC is to promote development cooperation and other policies so as to contribute to sustainable development, including pro-poor economic growth, poverty reduction, improvement of living standards in developing countries, and to a future in which no country will depend on aid.

The resolution of the Council on the mandate of the DAC provides the legal basis on the works of the DAC. The preamble shows the backgrounds for the need of DAC works and the main content (the decision) of the resolution provides the objective of the DAC works and the details of the mandate of the DAC for its role. The following sub-paragraphs provide the methodology as the boundary of its mandate for achieving the objectives. According to the resolution, the DAC shall do the following;

- monitor, assess, report, and promote the provision of resources that support sustainable development, as specified above, by collecting and analysing data and information on ODA and other official and private flows;
- review development co-operation policies and practices, particularly in relation to national and internationally agreed objectives and targets, and promote mutual learning;
- provide analysis, guidance and good practice to assist its Members and the expanded donor community to

enhance the quality and effectiveness of development assistance, particularly regarding pro-poor economic growth and poverty reduction;

- analyse and help shape the rapidly evolving global development architecture to optimise development results.
- promote perspectives on global public goods and policy coherence for development in coordination with other policy communities in OECD;
- engage or invite non-Member countries - in particular those with major development cooperation programmes - international organizations, private sector organizations, and civil society representatives, so as to assure the relevance and inclusiveness of DAC's work.

Therefore, the DAC is a committee which covers development areas amid all the areas that the OECD covers. In order to continue their common efforts, DAC should align development cooperation with global economy and must be aware of the risk of increasing marginalization of LDCs. Since DAC's work is not achievable without other policy communities and development stake holders, sustainable development of developing countries will be able to be achieved by developing countries continuous requirements of ODA.

4. The Development and ODA Issues In The OECD/DAC

As mentioned before, the DCD draw on knowledge and experience across the world and advise on diverse development policy issues, including: aid for trade, conflict and fragility, environment, gender equality, governance and poverty reduction

The committee architecture of the DAC's subsidiary bodies is shown in this organigram. The key topics of the work programs of the nine DAC subsidiary bodies are provided in the following pages.

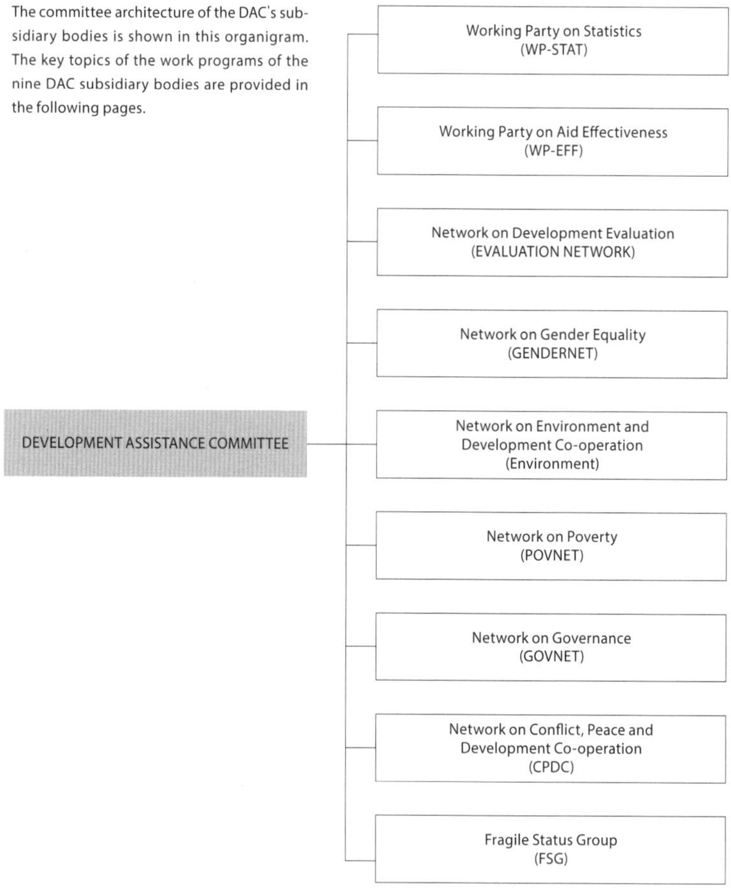

so as to improve development policies. The DAC is running 8 different subsidiary bodies that help DAC achieve improvement in development on those issues. Each issue has a network to collect and share knowledge and experience across the world. The following organigramme is the architecture of the DAC's subsidiary bodies.

• Environment and Development

The Network on Environment and Development Cooperation (ENVIRONET) of the DAC promotes and facilitates the integration of environment and climate change into all aspects of development works. The ENVIRONET formulates specific guidance for development co-operation efforts in support of environment and sustainable development, provides its members with a policy forum for sharing experience and disseminating good practice with regard to the integration of environmental concerns in development cooperation. Representatives from civil society and developing countries also participate as observers and help to support the networks' objectives. ENVIRONET builds on the knowledge, experience and practice of its members and participants. ENVIRONET supports developing countries' policies and efforts to promote environmentally-sustainable, resource-efficient livelihoods, and economies that are resilient to climate change. It seeks to enhance the impact of DAC policy advice and guidance on environment, green growth and climate change by promoting its dissemination and take-up.

• Aid effectiveness

In the 1960s, development resources surged. However, it became clear that this increase in funds was not resulting in the expected tangible improvements in people's lives. In the early-2000s, the formulation of the MDGs gave increasing impetus to the need to make aid more effective more quickly; without effective aid, the MDGs would not be achieved. In 2005, various initiatives to improve the impact of aid - such as encouraging donors to harmonize their funding and efforts and for both donors and recipients to use and strengthen the country's own systems - were brought together under the Paris Declaration on Aid Effectiveness which set out five principles for aid effectiveness. In 2008, **the Accra Agenda for Action** (AAA) reiterated the Paris principles and set out three further pillars around which to concentrate efforts.

The DAC's Working Party on Aid Effectiveness (WP-EFF) is the international partnership of donors and partner countries hosted by the DAC which works on improving the effectiveness of aid for greater impact on development and poverty reduction. Its current mandate is to promote, facilitate and monitor the implementation of the Paris Declaration on Aid Effectiveness endorsed by over 100 donors and developing countries at the High Level Forum held in March 2005.

• Evaluation of development programmes

DAC also has a subsidiary body of evaluation which name is EVALUATION NETWORK. The mandate of the DAC Network on Development Evaluation is to: strengthen the exchange of information, experience and cooperation on evaluation among network members. Strong and independent evaluation of development programmes provides information about what works, what does not and why. This learning contributes to improving the development effectiveness of aid and helps hold donors and partner country governments accountable for results. As a platform for evaluation learning and coordination, the Evaluation Network develops shared norms and standards and facilitates our members' efforts towards joint work by encouraging them to share and coordinate their plans for future evaluations.

• Conflict and fragility

Fragility and conflict negatively affect the lives of millions and pose a pressing challenge to ensure a safer and more equitable world for developed and developing countries alike. So as to cover areas of those conflicts and fragility, DAC organized a network. The International Network on Fragility and Conflict (INCAF) is a subsidiary body of the DAC. INCAF was founded in 2009 out of the merger of the former DAC Fragile States Group (FSG) and the DAC network on Conflict, Peace and Development

Cooperation (CPDC).

• Governance and development

The DAC Network on Governance (GovNet) brings together governance practitioners and experts to explore and promote more effective governance in developing countries. Since its creation in 1995, the DAC GovNet has provided members with a forum to exchange experiences and lessons, identify and disseminate what has worked where and why, and develop policy, analytical tools and operational approaches. GovNet has served as an incubator for cutting-edge processes such as the DAC work on fragile states, political economy analysis, accountability and democratic governance and work on anti-corruption. GovNet is a subsidiary body of the OECD DAC. The network focuses on two main work areas, 1) accountability and anti-corruption, 2) exploring better and different ways for development assistance providers to do their work.

• Gender equality and women's empowerment

The DAC Network on Gender Equality Contributes to improving the quality and effectiveness of development co-operation. The GENDERNET works to ensure that practice and implementation match global and national commitments to gender equality and women's empowerment in advancing economic, social and political development in partner countries. It is responsive to changing contexts and development priorities.

• Poverty reduction

The DAC Network on Poverty Reduction focuses on the multidimensionality of poverty and on the relationship between inequality, economic growth and poverty reduction in developing countries. POVNET provides a forum for the exchange of experience and best practice on pro-poor growth, i.e. involving the poor in generating growth and benefiting from it. It promotes the pursuit of the Millennium Development Goals.

• Aid for Trade

Selection of the DAC's activities includes **Aid for Trade**. The 2005 WTO Ministerial Meeting in Hong Kong mandated the operationalization of Aid for Trade. Subsequently, the OECD, in partnership with the WTO, established a monitoring system that encourages enhanced scrutiny and dialogue with the objective of delivering more and better Aid for Trade. History has shown that openness to trade is a key ingredient for economic success and raising living standards. The monitoring framework, which WTO in collaboration with the OECD has created, tracks progress in implementing the Aid for Trade Initiative in order to enhance its credibility. As a tool it is best characterized as a spotlight.

Lecture 6.
ODA and MDBs

1. Multinational Development Banks (MDBs)

2. The World Bank

3. The IDA (International Development Association) Agreement

ODA and MDBs

1. Multinational Development Banks(MDBs)

• **Overview**

When governments and international bodies suggest rationales on Official Development Assistance practiced across different countries, several laws are specified on proposals to support their actions. Each government and organization has its own rules, and the rules generally include articles on international development of their bodies. In addition, international development law established by various international organizations specify the identity such as roles, characters, organizations, and others so that the body makes promises on proper issues on a global level. The laws are mainly applied to states and international organizations on the issues of development. Those laws are also cited by governments that would like to set new rules regarding ODA works, affecting the higher law.

Major international organizations that enact such international development laws are: United Nations Development Programme (UNDP), United Nations Educational, Scientific and Cultural Organization (UNESCO), United Nations Conference on Trade and Development (UNCTAD), World Trade Organization (WTO), Development Cooperation Directorate and Committee (DCD/DAC) in OECD, International Development Association (IDA), World Bank, Asian Development Bank (ADB). In this section, explanation on the basic concept on what Multinational Development Banks (MDBs) are and what they do will be presented first. Next comes the information on the World Bank group among those MDBs. Then, International Development Association (IDA), which belongs World Bank Group, will be reviewed in detail based on its laws.

• Introduction to the MDBs

Multilateral Development Banks (MDBs) are institutions created by multiple groups of countries, providing financial assistance, usually in forms of loans and grants to developing countries. The purpose of their existence is to promote economic and social development to the recipient countries. The well-known examples of an MDB are the World Bank, the African Development Bank (AfDB), the Asian Development Bank (ADB), The European Bank of Reconstruction and Development (EBRD), and the Inter-American Development Bank (IDB).

MDBs typically take part in aiding investment projects and provide policy based loans. The investment loans they provide include not only huge infrastructure projects such as ports, highways or power plants, but other social projects concerning health and education as well. Meanwhile, the policy based loans are operated in a conditional manner. In other words, it would provide financing to a government if the government accepts a particular policy reform suggested by the institution. The policy reforms can be a change in any economic, social policy, or an implementation of a new policy. Once a project has proceeded with the financing that MDBs decided to provide, MDBs take evaluations on economic situations of beneficiaries and check effects of the ODA project. Those actions are done not only between parties that are directly involved, but also with member states of MDBs and other parties in the international society.

2. The World Bank

• Introduction and History

The World Bank is the largest, and the oldest existing MDB. The World Bank started with the Bretton Woods Conference, which was held in New Hampshire, United States in 1944. This meeting was held in order to regulate the international monetary and financial order after the World War II. The World Bank was created through the conference, along with institutions such as the International Monetary Fund (IMF).

The World Bank is a vital source of financial and technical assistance to developing countries around the world. Its main goal is to reduce poverty and support development throughout the world. In order to meet this goal, it offers low interest loans and zero to low interest credits to developing countries. They also provide and facilitate financing through fund partnerships with bilateral, multilateral donors. Next to financial support, they also provide policy advice, research and analysis, and technical assistance.

• Inside Institutions and their works

The World Bank Group comprises of three sub-institutions that make loans and grants to developing countries: the International Bank for Reconstruction and Development (IBRD), the International Development Association (IDA), and the International Finance Corporation (IFC). IFC is the affiliate for providing loans and equity investment on the private sector development, while the other two bodies are for international development on the public sector by providing concessional loan to the poorest countries. Other than those 3 bodies, there are two more sub-organizations: the Multilateral investment Guarantee Agency (MIGA) and the International Centre for the Settlement of Investment Disputes (ICSID). Focusing on aids which are classified as official development assistance, IBRD and IDA play the main role of providing concessional loans and grants. Further descriptions on the two institutions are below,

International Bank for Reconstruction and Development (IBRD)

The International Bank of Reconstruction and Development (IBRD), was the first World Bank affiliate created, and its articles of agreement became effective in 1945 with the signatures of 28 member governments. Today, the IBRD has near universal membership with 187 member nations. The IBRD gives non-concessional loans and loan guarantees as a type of financing. The types of borrowers of these kinds of provision usually are the middle income governments, and often some creditworthy low income countries.

International Development Association (IDA)

The IDA, however, provides interest-free loans and grants to the governments of the poorest countries with the main purpose of reducing poverty in these recipient countries. The IDA was established based on the need for a program to provide lending to the poor countries in the early 1950s. Initially, a plan for a lending program backed by multilateral donors was made in the reports from the United Nations with the support from the United States government. After initial deliberations, the idea to create the International Development Association was brought up within the bank (IBRD, or the World Bank).

As the initiative of the creation of IDA was brought up, after consultations, which began among the member governments of the World Bank in 1958, the Bank's Board of Governors, at its Annual Meeting in 1959, approved a United States resolution calling on the Bank's Executive Directors to draft the Articles of Agreement for IDA, which will be discussed more later on in this chapter.

IDA provides highly concessional loans, which means that IDA credits carry no or low interest charges. The lending decision is made according to the recipient countries' risk of debt distress, the level of GNI per capita, and the credit worthiness for the International Bank for Reconstruction and Development borrowing. The countries with a high rate of debt distress receive 100 percent of their financial assistance in the form of grants, while the recipient countries with a medium risk of debt distress receive 50 percent in the form of grants. Repayment of concessional loans is stretched over 25 to 40 years, including a 5 to 10-year grace period.

3. The IDA (International Development Association) Agreement

• Background

The International Development Association was established in 1960. IDA is operated in accordance with the IDA agreement that became effective on September 24, 1960. The purpose of its creation was to improve mutual cooperation for constructive economic purposes, for the stable development of the world economy, and for a balanced growth of international trade with the fostering of international relationships. The IDA Agreement, which constitutes the reason for the foundation of IDA includes provisions on the purpose and work of the institution, rights and obligation of the institution, operations, amendments, and other issues.

< The IDA Agreement Articles>

Introductory Article
Article 1. Purpose
Article 2. Membership, Initial Subscription
Article 3. Additions to Resources
Article 4. Currencies
Article 5. Operations
Article 6. Organization and Management
Article 7. Withdrawal: Suspension of Membership; Suspension of Operations

Article 8. Status, Immunities and Privileges
Article 9. Amendments
Article 10. Interpretation and Arbitration
Article 11. Final Provisions
Schedule A. Initial Subscriptions

- **Details of the Agreement**

Article I: Purposes

IDA Agreement starts with specifying the institution's purpose in the first place. Looking through article 1, the purpose of the IDA is to focus on the issues of international development cooperation. Goals of the cooperation are written as to promote economic development, increase productivity, and raise the standard of living of less-developed countries. Also, the institution provides finance to meet their goals to the beneficiaries. One of the forms of finance they provide is conventional loans, and shares the same values with IBRD while the association supports their activities.

> The purposes of the Association are to promote economic development, increase productivity and thus raise standards of living in the less-developed areas of the world included within the Association's membership, in particular by providing finance to meet their important developmental requirements on terms which

are more flexible and bear less heavily on the balance of payments than those of conventional loans, thereby furthering the developmental objectives of the International Bank for Reconstruction and Development (hereinafter called "the Bank") and supplementing its activities. The Association shall be guided in all its decisions by the provisions of this Article.

Article II: Membership, Initial, Subscriptions
Section 1. Membership
Section 2. Initial Subscriptions
Section 3. Limitation on Liability

Section 1 of Article 2 provides information on who the members of IDA are. Membership is based on the World Bank membership. Membership is also opened to other members of the Bank for the future.

Section 2. Initial Subscriptions
- Upon accepting membership, each member shall subscribe funds in the amount assigned to it. Such subscriptions are herein referred to as initial subscriptions.
- Ten percent of the initial subscription of each original member shall be payable in gold or freely convertible currency …

Section 2 explains one of the basic responsibilities of membership subscriptions. Bracket C and D provide the details of the subscriptions. Members listed in schedule A should fulfill its initial subscription, which is 10% of the entire mandatory subscription. The other 90% of subscriptions is payable later. 10% of the initial subscription of each original member is payable in gold or so-called 'freely convertible currency'. 'Freely convertible currency' written in bracket C means currency of a member which the Association determines with the consultation of the International Monetary Fund (IMF). The currency, once recognized as free convertible, can be adequately changeable into the currencies of other members for the purposes of the Association's operations. Other than the association office authority, members can also determine such determination of currencies.

Article 2, in short, describes the basic structure of the membership in a financial perspective, using the expression of 'subscriptions of members'

Article III: Additions to resources

Section 1. Additional Subscriptions

Section 2. Supplementary Resources Provided by a Member in the Currency of Another Member

Section 1. Additional Subscriptions

- The Association shall at such time as it deems appropriate in the light of the schedule for completion of

> payments on initial subscriptions of original members, and at intervals of approximately five years thereafter, review the adequacy of its resources and, if it deems desirable, shall authorize a general increase in subscriptions. ··· Subscriptions pursuant to this Section are herein referred to as additional subscriptions.

In the Article 2, we could briefly understand what the 'subscriptions' and 'initial subscriptions' are. Subscriptions are classified into 2 categories by its order and proportion, and first the 10% that the members pay for its fulfillment of obligation is called 'initial subscriptions.' In Article 3 section 1, there is a definition of 'additional subscriptions' which take the last 90% of subscription after members pay their initial subscription. After IDA regards one's initial subscription as proper resources, it approves a general increase in subscription. This increased amount is referred to as 'additional subscription.' How the Association decides whether the initial subscription's adequacy is divided into 2 ways. The possibility is evaluated either by the Association or by the votes of members. In terms of vote, more than two-thirds of the total voting power enables to allow the collection of additional amounts.

Article IV: Currencies

Section 1. Use of Currencies

Section 2. Maintenance of Value of Currency Holdings

Section 1. Use of Currencies

(a) Currency of any member listed in Part II of Schedule A, … may be used by the Association for administrative expenses incurred by the Association in the territories of such member and, insofar as consistent with sound monetary policies, in payment for goods and services produced in the territories of such member and required for projects financed by the Association and located in such territories; and in addition when and to the extent justified by the economic and financial situation of the member concerned as determined by agreement between the member and the Association, such currency shall be freely convertible or otherwise usable for projects financed by the Association and located outside the territories of the member.

Subscriptions collected by IDA's members are used in various ways, and Article 4 stipulates the usage of the currencies. Firstly, the money is used for the administration of the association in addition to the execution of its monetary policies. Goods and services required for projects financed by the Association are also paid by its budget. Furthermore, it is possible to use the money for its member country with agreement of member states and the association. The usability of currencies received by the association in payment of subscriptions and as supplementary resources are governed by the terms of the arrangements pursuant to which such currencies are received. It shall not be subject to any restriction by the member.

Section 2 in Article 4 describes the way the association maintains the values of the currencies of subscriptions. In the case the value of a member's currency is reduced, the member should pay its additional amount of currencies enough to maintain the value. Vice versa, if there's an increase in value of certain member's currency, the association returns its additional profit equal to the increase in value to the member country. Waiver by the association is possible when a uniform proportionate change in the par value of the currencies of all its member is made by the International Monetary Fund. In case of the deflation of value of currency holdings, added currency by corresponding members is convertible and usable to the same extent as such currency. Formerly this property of currency in the association is referred to as 'freely convertible.'

Article V: operations

Section 1. Use of Resources and Conditions of Financing

Section 2. Form and Terms of Financing

Section 3. Modifications of Terms of Financing

Section 4. Cooperation with Other International Organizations and Members Providing Development Assistance

Section 5. Miscellaneous Operations

Section 6. Political Activity Prohibited

Section 1. Use of Resources and Conditions of Financing

The Association shall provide financing to further development in the less-developed areas of the world included within the Association's membership.

Operation of fund formed in IDA is specified in Article 5. According to Section 1 in the article, specific projects funded by the Association take the priority of using IDA's resources. The association shall not provide financing services if such financing is available from private sources in certain projects. In general, the member country in whose territories the project is located is subject to such financing after a careful feasibility study.

Form of financing usually takes the form of loans. The financial assistances from IDA require such type of loan. Such financing has a long term repayment period, and the interest is considerably low compared to regular loans. It usually has specific terms and conditions on reimbursement. In some cases, guarantees of government are ensured on some loans. Section 4 allows the possibility of cooperation with other international organizations and members providing development assistance. Section 6 speculates that political activities supported by IDA's finance are not permitted.

Article VI: Organization and management

Section 1. Structure of the Association:

Board of Governors, Executive Directors, President, Officers and Staffs

Section 2. Board of Governors

Section 3. Voting

Section 4. Executive Directors

Section 5. President and Staff

Section 6. Relationship to the Bank

Section 7. Relations with Other International Organizations

Section 8. Location of Offices

Section 9. Depositories

Section 10. Channel of Communication

Section 11. Publication of Reports and Provision of Information

Section 12. Disposition of Net Income

Article 6 comprises of 12 sections. Section 1 depicts the structure of the association. The main bodies of association have 4 parts, which are a board of governors, the executive directors, a president, other officers and staffs. Section 2 describes what the board of governors is. As described in the section, all the powers of the association is vested in the board of governors. So the final decision making body is the board. It consists of the governors appointed by a member of the IBRD. It may delegate to the executive directors authority to exercise its powers. But the director cannot represent the authority of the appointment of new members. Section 4 is about the executive directors. Executive directors of IDA are responsible for the conduct of the general operations of the Association.

> Section 3. Voting
>
> Each original member shall, in respect of its initial subscription, have 500 votes plus one additional vote for each $5,000 of its initial subscription. Subscriptions other than initial subscriptions of original members shall carry such voting rights as the Board of Governors shall determine pursuant to the provisions of Article II
>
> ...

In section 3, how voting power of each member is decided is stated. Briefly explained, the more amount a member contributes to the association there is, the more voting power they exercise. Members who basically suffice its condition of initial subscription have 500 votes and then every $5,000 grants 1 more vote. Decisions on issues dealt in IDA are concluded by a majority of the votes each member cast. Section 5 states the identity of the president. In principle, the president has no right of casting a vote when it comes to decision-making. However, if there's equal division on favor and oppose, the president has the right of selection. The president participates in meetings of the board of governors plus acting as a chief of the operating association's staff.

Section 6 and 7 determines the relationships with associated organizations, while section 8 explains the location of headquarters of IDA. Section 9 confines depositories of their currencies to the central banks of the members. Section 10 sets the communication channel with the bank, which is mainly each member's administrative office dealing similar issues with the association. According to section 11, the association releases annual reports and reports on the operation every year. Lastly, section 12 states that if there's net income it is on the hands of the board of governors.

Article VII: Withdrawal; suspension of membership; suspension of operations

Section 1. Withdrawal by Members

Section 2. Suspension of Membership

Section 3. Suspension or Cessation of Membership in

the Bank
Section 4. Rights and Duties of Governments Ceasing to be Members
Section 5. Suspension of Operations and Settlement of Obligations

- If a member fails to fulfill any of its obligations to the Association, the Association may suspend its membership by decision of a majority of the Governors, exercising a majority of the total voting power. The member so suspended shall automatically cease to be a member one year from the date of its suspension unless a decision is taken by the same majority to restore the member to good standing.

Among the sections in Article 7, to be noticeable is section 2, stating in terms of suspension of membership. The association is able to put on hold member's membership using its authority, in the way of voting of member countries or decision of the board. The member decided on to lose its membership automatically siezes its membership after 1 year, unless the same majority votes for the restoration of membership in a vote.

Article VIII: Status, Immunities and Privileges

Section 1. Purposes of Article

Section 2. Status of the Association

Section 3. Position of the Association with Regard to Judicial Process

Section 4. Immunity of Assets from Seizure

Section 5. Immunity of Archives

Section 6. Freedom of Assets from Restrictions

Section 7. Privilege for Communications

Section 8. Immunities and Privileges of Officers and Employees

Section 9. Immunities from Taxation

Section 10. Application of Article

SECTION 3. Position of the Association with Regard to Judicial Process

Actions may be brought against the Association only in a court of competent jurisdiction in the territories of a member in which the Association has an office, has appointed an agent for the purpose of accepting service or notice of process, or has issued or guaranteed securities. No actions shall, however, be brought by members or persons acting for or deriving claims from members. The property and assets of the Association shall, wheresoever located and by whomsoever held, be immune from all forms of seizure, attachment or execution before the delivery of final judgment against the Association

Article 8 states the status, immunities and privileges of the association in the territories of each member. According to the article, the association has full juridical personality as to contract, to acquire and dispose of immovable and movable property, and to institute legal proceedings. Section 3 of the article notes that property and asset of the association shall be immune from all forms of seizure, attachment or execution before the delivery of final judgments against association. Also, association's office in a member country cannot be applied for other member country's jurisdiction. Things that have independency from other member countries that have association's branch are not only properties and assets. Archives have freedom, and communication with other groups within territory is ensured. Officers and employees of the association are also immune to other countries as well as taxation.

ARTICLE IX: AMENDMENTS

If there's any proposal to modify this agreement, the bill will be brought to the board of directors. In the meeting, when three-fifths of the members, having four-fifths of the total voting power, have accepted the proposed amendments, the proposal passes and is addressed to all members.

ARTICLE X: INTERPRETATION AND ARBITRATION

In case there is any question on interpreting provisions of this agreement, the inquiry shall be submitted to the executive directors for their decision. In terms of arbitration, unless the conflict caused by disagreement between the association and a country which temporary lost its membership is not settled within the association, such disagreement shall be submitted to arbitration by a tribunal of three arbitrators.

ARTICLE XI: FINAL PROVISIONS

Section 1. Entry into Force
Section 2. Signature
Section 3. Territorial Application
Section 4. Inauguration of the Association
Section 5. Registration

The final provisions have other rules on the regulations of the membership or the organization. They are related to the entry into force, the signature and the application of this international development law.

Lecture 7.
IBRD, ADB, and AFDB

1. World Bank
2. Agreement of the International Bank for Reconstruction and Development (IBRD)
3. Asian Development Bank (ADB)
4. The Structure of the ADB Agreement
5. The African Development Bank (AfDB) and Its Related Laws

IBRD, ADB, and AFDB

1. World Bank

MDBs that this chapter embraces are World Bank, ADB and AfDB. They are working as international public banks for development works, operated by international members. Such international members consist of states around the globe, and possibly institutions co-founded by several countries. What do the MDBs do? First, they carry out conventional task as general bank. They have monetary authority for reservation and loans. Second, MDBs, as banks that work for the international development issues, raise funds for development projects and make investments for their goals. Third, they undertake evaluations of economic situations and effects of states and ODA project. Those works are usually done in association with member states of MDBs and others in the international society.

• **The inside institutions in the World Bank**

The World Bank Group has two unique development institutions: the International Development Association (IDA) and International Bank of Reconstruction and Development (IBRD). Those two institutions carry out projects related to international development in the public sector. The International Finance Corporation (IFC), which is also a member of World Bank group, takes in charge of private sector development. Besides, there are two additional members of the World Bank Group: the Multilateral Investment Guarantee Agency (MIGA), the International Centre for the Settlement of Investment Disputes (ICSID).

IBRD and IDA support different kind of countries divided by their economic status. IBRD provides the credit which is also said in other words as loans to governments of middle-income and creditworthy low-income countries, whereas IDA provides its interest-free loans and grants to governments of the poorest countries. How they speculates one's economic status depends on categories on its own.

2. Agreement of the International Bank for Reconstruction and Development (IBRD)

• Overview

Agreement of the International Bank for Reconstruction and Development (IBRD) is the main law for the regulation of the IBRD. The structure, management and other activities of the Bank are based on this law. The articles and the schedules of the IBRD Agreement are as below;

Article 1. Purposes
Article 2. Membership In and Capital of the Bank
Article 3. General Provisions Relating to Loans And Guarantees
Article 4. Operations
Article 5. Organization and Management
Article 6. Withdrawal and Suspension of Membership: Suspension Of Operations
Article 7. Status, Immunities, And Previleges
Article 8. Amendments
Article 9. Interpretation
Article 10. Approval Deemed Given

• Details of the Agreement

Article I: Purposes

The first article gives five purposes of the establishment of the bank. According to the first article, the purposes of IBRD are: 1. to assist in the reconstruction and development by facilitating the investment of capital, 2. to promote private foreign investment by means of guarantees or participations in loans and other investments, 3. to promote the long-range balanced growth of international trade and the maintenance of equilibrium in balances of payments, 4. to arrange the loans through other channels, 5. to conduct its operations in order to assist in bringing about a smooth transition from a wartime to a peacetime economy.

Article II: Membership in and capital of the bank

Article II on the membership and the capital issues of the Bank consists of 10 sections as below;

Section 1. Membership
Section 2. Authorised Capital
Section 3. Subscription of Shares
Section 4. Issue Price of Shares
Section 5. Division and Calls of Subscribed Capital
Section 6. Limitation on Liability
Section 7. Method of Payment of Subscriptions for Shares

Section 8. Time of Payment of Subscriptions

Section 9. Maintenance of Value of Currency Holdings of the Bank

Section 10. Restriction on Disposal of Shares

Article III: General provisions relating to loans and guarantees

Article III is on the general regulations of the loans and the guarantees from the Bank. The provisions of the article are the legal frameworks for the procedures of the works. The sections consist of 6 sections as below;

Section 1. Use of Resources

Section 2. Dealings between Members and the Bank

Section 3. Limitations on Guarantees and Borrowings of the Bank

Section 4. Conditions on which the Bank may Guarantee or make Loans

Section 5. Use of Loans Guaranteed, Participated in or made by the Bank

Section 6. Loans to the International Finance Corporation

Article IV: Operations

10 sections of Article IV provide the detailed rules on the operation of the works as below;

Section 1. Methods Making or Facilitating Loans

Section 2. Availability and Transferability of Currencies

Section 3. Provision of Currencies for Direct Loans

Section 4. Payment Provisions for Direct Loans

Section 5. Guarantees

Section 6. Special Reserve

Section 7. Methods of Meeting Liabilities of the Bank in Case of Defaults

Section 8. Miscellaneous Operations

Section 9. Warning to be placed on Securities

Section 10. Political Activity prohibited

Article V: Organisation and management

The provisions of the Article V are on the structure of the Bank and its management regulations. They are many rules for the framework of the Bank, main bodies, voting systems, offices and even management of the money in the Bank. They consist of 14 sections as below;

Section 1. Structure of the Bank

Section 2. Board of Governors

Section 3. Voting

Section 4. Executive Directors

Section 5. President and Staff

Section 6. Advisory Council

Section 7. Loan Committees

Section 8. Relationship to other International Organisations

Section 9. Location of Offices

Section 10. Regional Offices and Council

Section 11. Depositories

Section 12. Form of Holdings of Currency

Section 13. Publication of Reports and Provision of Information

Section 14. Allocation of Net Income

Article VI: Withdrawal and suspension of membership: suspension of operations

5 sections of Article VI provide the detailed regulations on the membership of the Bank. If a Member cannot fulfill the requirements, the Bank will do certain actions for the work based on this regulation. The sections are as below;

Section 1. Right of Members to Withdraw

Section 2. Suspension of Membership

Section 3. Cessation of Membership in International Monetary Fund

Section 4. Settlement of Accounts with Governments Ceasing to be Members

Section 5. Suspension of Operations and Settlement of Obligations

Article VII: Status, immunities and privileges

The provisions of this article are on the status of the Bank in international society. According to the provision, the Bank has legal personality and it can do various types of legal activities including a judicial process. Furthermore, the Bank has several kinds of special status or privileges for the functions of the Bank. These privileges are also provided to the staffs for their works. The sections are 10 as below;

Section 1. Purposes of Article
Section 2. Status of the Bank
Section 3. Position of the Bank with Regard to Judicial Process
Section 4. Immunity of Assets from Seizure
Section 5. Immunity of Archives
Section 6. Freedom of Assets from Restrictions
Section 7. Privilege for Communications
Section 8. Immunities and Privileges of Officers and Employees
Section 9. Immunities from Taxation
Section 10. Application of Article

Other articles

Other Articles are ARTICLE VIII (AMENDMENTS), ARTICLE IX (INTERPRETATION), ARTICLE X (APPROVAL DEEMED GIVEN) and ARTICLE XI (FINAL PROVISIONS). The final article consists of 3 sections (SECTION 1: Entry into Force, SECTION 2: Signature and SECTION 3: Inauguration of the Bank). Then this law has two sub-rules, schedules (SCHEDULE A: SUBSCRIPTIONS and SCHEDULE B: ELECTION OF EXECUTIVE DIRECTORS).

3. Asian Development Bank (ADB)

• Background

Asian Development Bank (ADB) was established on 22nd August 1966 to facilitate economic development of countries in Asia. The foundation is mainly led by US and Japan, followed by the members of the United Nations Economic and Social Commission for Asia and the Pacific (UNESCAP) and non-regional developed countries. The bank started with 31 members, and increased its number to 67 by now. 48 members are from the Asia-Pacific region and 19 members are from other regions. At the very first phase of its foundation, ADB modeled its structure similar to the World Bank Group. The bank adopted similar weighted voting system, where the voting power is granted in proportion with member's capital subscription. As indicated above that US and Japan were the main members of ADB, two countries have 552,210 shares each, being the largest proportion of shares among member countries.

• Sectors and Themes of ADB's activities

The ADB, as a multilateral development finance institution, provides loans, technical assistance and grants. The clients of the institution are the member state governments and also the shareholders of the Bank.

The main areas in which the operations of the ADB focus are inclusive economic growth, environmentally sustainable growth, and regional integration. The ADB employs its resource in the areas where it has comparative strength as the following areas show; Infrastructure (water, energy, transport, urban development, information and communications technology), Environment, Information of Communication and Technology, Finance sector development, Education, Health, Agriculture and natural resources, and Public sector management.

Based on those sectors, ADB has its themes which fit with goals featured above (economic growth, sustainable environmental growth, and regional integration.) Those themes are in line with the United Nations MDGs and SDGs, which are: Capacity Development, Climate Change, Environmental Sustainability, Gender and Development, Governance, Poverty Reduction, Private Sector Development, Social Development, Urban Development.

• Financing Operations

Three financing sectors are driven by ADB. Firstly, public sector financing helps governments and public sector entities such as state-owned enterprises, using the tools of loan, technical assistance, and grants. Private sector financing provides direct financial assistance to private sector projects as a catalyst for private investments. Further special funds are operated for specific subjects and targets such as "Afghanistan Infrastructure Trust Fund' and 'Japan Special Fund'.

4. The Structure of the ADB Agreement

• Framework of the agreement

Agreement of the Asian Development Bank (ADB) is the main law for the regulation of the ADB. The structure, management and other activities of the Bank are based on this law. The agreement consists of 10 chapters with 66 articles. The 10 Chapters of the ADB agreement are as below;

Chapter 1. Purpose, Functions and Membership
Chapter 2. Capital
Chapter 3. Operations
Chapter 4. Borrowing and Other Miscellaneous Powers
Chapter 5. Currencies
Chapter 6. Organization and Management
Chapter 7. Withdrawal and Suspension of Members,

Temporary Suspension and Termination of Operations of the Bank

Chapter 8. Status, Immunities, Exemptions and Privileges

Chapter 9. Amendments, Interpretation, Arbitration

Chapter 10. Final Provisions

• CHAPTER I and II

Chapter I consists of three articles. The articles provide basic rules for the issue of Purpose, Functions and Membership. Article 1 specifies that the purpose of ADB is: 1. to foster economic growth and co-operation in the region of Asia and the Far East, and 2. to contribute to the acceleration of the process of economic development of the developing member countries.

Then, Article 2 presents the function of the ADB complying with the bank's purpose written in Article 1. To sum up, the main function of the bank is: 1) to promote investment in the region of public and private capital for development purposes, 2) to utilize the resources at its disposal for financing development of the developing member countries, and 3) to meet requests from members in the region to assist them in the co-ordination of their development policies and plans. 4) to provide technical assistance for preparation, financing and execution of development projects and programmes, 5) to cooperate with the United Nations and other international institutions, as well as national entities whether public or private, 6) to undertake such other activities.

Then, Chapter II is on the capital of the Bank. Four articles in this chapter provide the various types of resources for the capital of the Bank.

• CHAPTER III OPERATIONS

Chapter III is on the general works of the Bank. The 13 articles (Article 8-20) in the chapter provide the regulations and limitations of the operations of the Bank as stated below:

Article 8. Use of Resources
Article 9. Ordinary and Special Operations
Article 10. Separation of Operations
Article 11. Recipients and Methods of Operation
Article 12. Limitations on Ordinary Operations
Article 13. Provision of Currencies for Direct Loans
Article 14. Operating Principles
Article 15. Terms and Conditions for Direct Loans and Guarantees
Article 16. Commission and Fees
Article 17. Special Reserve
Article 18. Methods of Meeting Liabilities of the Bank
Article 19. Special Funds
Article 20. Special Funds Resources

• CHAPTER IV and V

Chapter IV and V are the articles on the regulations of the powers and the currencies. The articles are as below;

Chapter 4. Borrowing And Other Miscellaneous Powers
Article 21. General Powers
Article 22. Notice to be Placed on Securities

Chapter 5 Currencies
Article 23. Determination of Convertibility
Article 24. Use of Currencies
Article 25. Maintenance of Value of the Currency Holding of the Bank

• CHAPTER VI ORGANIZATION AND MANAGEMENT

By reviewing Chapter VI in the agreement, the structure of the department where comprehensive decision and management of the bank's purpose is made can be understood. According to Article 26, managerial entities comprise of 3 bodies, which are the board of governors, board of directors, and the president. The board of governors is the highest policy-making body of ADB. It is composed of one representative from each member state. Article 27, 28 and 29 provide the regulations on the board of governors as below;

Article 27. Board of Governors: Composition
Article 28. Board of Governors: Powers
Article 29. Board of Governors: Procedure

Article 30, 31 and 32 provide the regulations on the Board of Directors. The board consists of 12 members pulled out from the board of governors. Directors are elected among governors who ranked the highest 12 members by vote within the board. There is regional quota in the places, 8 members from Asia-Pacific members and 4 from non-regional members. Article 30 to 32 on this issue are stated below;

Article 30. Board of Directors: Composition
Article 31. Board of Directors: Powers
Article 32. Board of Directors: Procedure

Article 34 is on the President. The president is acting as the chairperson of the Board of Directors and managers of the ADB. The person is elected by the Board of Governors, working for five years with the possibility of a re-election. So far, the president has always been Japanese, showing the country's influence on the bank. The other regulations on the management of the organization are based on the articles from 35 to 40. The articles are bellows;

Article 35. Vice President(s)

Article 36. Prohibition of Political Activity: The International Character of The Bank
Article 37. Office of The Bank
Article 38. Channel of Communications, Depositories
Article 39. Working Language, Reports
Article 40. Allocation of Net Income

• CHAPTER VII and VIII

ADB can manage the works and membership based on Chapter VII. This chapter has several articles on the operation of the Bank and the membership as below;

Article 41. Withdrawal
Article 42. Suspension of Membership
Article 43. Settlement of Accounts
Article 44. Temporary Suspensions of Operations
Article 45. Termination of Operations
Article 46. Liability of Members and Payment of Claims
Article 47. Distribution of Assets

Chapter VIII describes the privileges for the bank and the staff. ADB staff basically has immunity on judicial proceedings, and freedom of handling assets and archives are bestowed. In addition, tax exemption is applied as a kind of privileges, also there is a privilege of communications with governments and institutions. Bank personnel who is directly or indirectly involved in bank operation, such as governors, directors, alternates, officers and employees have such immunities and privileges. The articles are as below;

Article 48. Purpose of Chapter
Article 49. Legal Status
Article 50. Immunity From Judicial Proceedings
Article 51. Immunity of Assets
Article 52. Immunity of Archives
Article 53. Freedom of Assets from Restrictions
Article 54. Privilege for Communications
Article 55. Immunities and Privileges of Bank Personnel
Article 56. Exemption from Taxation
Article 57. Implementation
Article 58. Waiver of Immunities, Exemptions and Privileges

• CHAPTER IX and X

The last two chapters are on the regulations of other issues, such as amendment and arbitration. Articles 59-66 of the chapters are as below;

Chapter 9. Amendments, Interpretation, Arbitration
Article 59. Amendments
Article 60. Interpretation or Application
Article 61. Arbitration
Article 62. Approval Deemed Given

Chapter 10. Final Provisions
Article 63. Signature and Deposit
Article 64. Ratification or Acceptance
Article 65. Entry into Force
Article 66. Commencement of Operations

5. The African Development Bank (AfDB) and Its Related Laws

• History and Works

The African Development Bank was established in 1964, in order to promote economic and social development in Africa. It is comprised of groups, including the African Development Bank (AfDB), the African Development Fund (ADF), and the Nigeria Trust Fund (NTF). The African Development Bank provides loans and grants to African governments and private companies investing in the regional member countries (RMC) in Africa. The Bank is owned and funded by the member governments, and has a public interest mandate to reduce poverty and promote sustainable development.

The Bank has four main functions. The first function is the loans and equity investments. The purpose of the function is the advancement, both social and economic, of the regional member countries (RMC). The second function is the technical assistance for the preparation and execution of development projects and programs. The last two functions are the investment of public and private capital for development purposes and the coordination of development policies and plans.

The two funds that are included in the Group are the African Development Fund (ADF) and the Nigeria Trust Fund (NTF). The ADF was established in 1972 for the purpose of financing development on concessional terms to low income RMCs which are unable to borrow on the non-concessional terms of the AfDB. The main aim of its activities was to harmonize its lending strategy with poverty reduction. The NTF was established in 1976 by the Nigerian Government, with a purpose to assist the development efforts of the poorest AfDB members and to provide financing for projects of national or regional importance.

• Agreement on establishing the African Development Bank

The law on the AfDB is in agreement with establishing the African Development Bank. The agreement has 60 articles on total, divided by 11 chapters and the mainframe of the law is similar to the ADB agreement. Chapters and articles of the ADB agreement are below;

Chapter 1. Definitions
Article 1
Chapter 2. Purpose and Participation
Article 2-3
Chapter 3. Resources
Article 4-10
Chapter 4. Currencies
Article 11-13
Chapter 5. Operations
Article 14-21

Chapter 6. Organization and Management

Article 22-36

Chapter 7. Withdrawal; Suspension of Participation; Termination of Operations

Article 37-40

Chapter 8. Status, Immunities, Exemptions and Privileges

Article 41-50

Chapter 9. Amendments

Article 51

Chapter 10. Interpretation and Arbitration

Article 52-53

Chapter 11. Final Provisions

Article 54-60

Lecture 8. Korean Economy and the ODA

1. The Korean Economy

2. The Korean ODA

3. The Structure of the Korean ODA

Korean Economy and the ODA

1. The Korean Economy

Korea was one of the world's fastest growing economies from the early 1960s to the late 1990s. As a result, currently, Korea is the 11th largest economy in the world. Such development based on the properly designed development strategies (adapting the export-oriented strategy) and effective use of foreign assistance and investments. Especially in the international trade stage, Korea is the seventh largest exporter and tenth largest importer in the world. Such rapid development of Korean economy so called as "The Miracle on the Han River". Before the "Miracle on the Han River", Korea was one of the poorest countries in the world.

• The Korean War

The Korean War was a war between North and South Korea,

in which the United Nations force led by the United States of America fought for the South, and China fought for the North, which was also assisted by the Soviet Union. The war arose from the division of Korea at the end of World War II and from global tensions of the Cold War that developed immediately afterwards.

Korea was ruled by Japan from 1910 until the closing days of World War II. After the 1945, the Soviet Union and the United States occupied Korea by north and south based on the 38th parallel. By 1948, two separate governments had been set up. Both governments claimed to be the legitimate government of Korea, and neither side accepted the border as permanent. The conflict escalated into open warfare when North Korean forces invaded South Korea on 25 June 1950. On that day, the UN Security Council recognized this North Korean act as invasion and called for an immediate ceasefire. Twenty-one countries of the UN eventually contributed to the defense of South Korea.

The fighting ended on 27 July 1953, when an armistice was signed. The agreement created the Korean Demilitarized Zone (DMZ) to separate North and South Korea, and allowed the return of prisoners. However, no peace treaty has been signed, and the two Koreas are technically still at war. Periodic clashes, many of which were deadly, have continued to the present.

• **The Economy of Korea after the War**

After Korean War, South Korea was one of the poorest countries in the world. South Korea's per-capita GNP was $82 in 1961. Moreover, South Korea had no natural resources and infrastructure and there was overpopulation in its small territory. So South Korea had to depend on foreign assistance. And such foreign assistance was the main source for financing the nation's deficit in the 1950s and early 1960s. During the 1950s and 1960s, more than 70% of Korea's imports were financed by foreign aid. Between 1945 and the early 1990s, Korea received a total assistance of $12.69 billion from the international community. Effective use of the enormous amount of foreign aid was crucial to Korea's sustained economic growth. The Korean government successfully utilized financial assistance to overcome various domestic challenges through state-led projects designed to spur economic development. As illustrated by the graph below, this aid was primarily provided by the United States, Japan and the European DAC members.

The Miracle on the Han River is a term used to refer to South Korea's postwar export-fueled economic growth, including rapid industrialization, technological achievement, education boom, large rise in living standards, rapid urbanization, skyscraper boom, modernization, successful hosting of the 1988 Summer Olympics and co-hosting of the 2002 FIFA World Cup. This growth was accompanied by a democratization and globalization that transformed the country from the destruction of the Korean War to a wealthy and developed country with a globally influential economy and prominent multinational companies.

More specifically, the term refers to the economic growth of Seoul, through which the Han River flows, although it is generally used in reference to the country as a whole. Also, the "miracle" generally refers to the period between 1961 and 1996. The phrase comes from the "Miracle on the Rhine", used to refer to the economic rebirth of West Germany after World War II, resulting partially from the Marshall Plan. The "Miracle on the Han" is used to refer to the growth of postwar South Korea into the world's 11th largest economy and a role model for many developing countries in Asia. Seoul's infrastructure was destroyed during the Korean War and millions lived in poverty at the time, with thousands of unemployed people struggling to fulfill basic needs. Korea had a per capita income of less than $80 per year in 1961. During that time, South Korea was mostly dependent on foreign aid.

In less than four decades, Seoul was transformed into a global city, a center of business and commerce in Northeast Asia and a highly developed economic hub, laying the grounds for an advanced technological and communications infrastructure. Koreans consider this rapid growth a symbol of national pride and self-sufficiency. Besides the Saemaul movement, the Korean government carried out another effective economic development plan called the Five-Year Economic Development Plan. There were more than five plans created, and they were designed to revive the economy. Each of the plans greatly contributed to industrialization and enlargement of the marketplaces of Korea.

- *Economic development during postwar governments (1953–1961)*

In the aftermath of the Korean War, South Korea became increasingly authoritarian as a result of militant anti-Communist policies enacted by President Lee Seungman. Despite these issues, the Lee administration is noted for at least two achievements that aided economic growth. First, Lee's firm leadership in the aftermath of the war allowed South Korea to stabilize itself. Secondly, the Lee administration implemented an important land reform that provided for the redistribution of land, averting a potentially explosive social issue. However, when Lee and the Liberal Party rigged the presidential election of 1960 in an attempt to consolidate their power, nationwide demonstrations led by angry students brought about the end of Lee's regime, to be succeeded democratically by Jang myeon, the leader of the Democratic Party. However, with factional and other differences, economic and social problems continued to mount. In 1961, a military coup led by General Park Junghee overthrew the Democratic Party, giving rise to a military junta.

- Economic development during Park Junghee rule (1961–1979)

One of the most important contributors to the "Miracle on the Han River" was the first Five Year Economic Development Plan announced by the Park Junghee government. It aimed to mobilize national resources in establishing a self-supporting industrial economy. "Treat employees like family" was Park's new motto, which also led to Korea's economic success. With this motto, Korean workers were claimed to be 2.5 times more productive than American workers even though Korean workers were paid one-tenth of American wages.

Park's rule is remembered by Koreans with mixed emotions. Many praise him for the contributions he made to Korea's economy and its recovery, but contemporary opinions criticize him for systematically disregarding human rights and censoring the media as part of a brutal military dictatorship. Following a military coup in the 1960s, Park established a strong authoritarian rule characterized by a one-party regime. In this authoritarian state, the leading party only had to appease a small constituency of the ruling or military elite.

During Park's tenure, Korea suffered from censorship in the press and media. Because of strong antipathies toward communism, Korean journalism and free speech were tightly controlled. Disregarding human rights and violations, Park utilized the abundant supply of cheap labor and place his foremost priority on Korea's economic restoration. Morality laws established mandatory curfews and regulations on attire and music. In his programme of 'Yushin Kaehyuk' (Revitalizing Reforms), he caused Korean cinema to enter into a moribund period considered by many to be the lowest periods in the history of Korean cinema.

Such enormous growth of economy came with costs to freedom. Although Park was successful in bringing economic recovery to Korea, he trampled on human rights and often imprisoned those who questioned his rule. Park believed that South Korea was neither ready to be a full democratic nation nor a free nation. As he stated, "Democracy cannot be realized without an economic revolution". Park argued that the poverty of the nation would make it vulnerable, and therefore an urgent task was to eliminate poverty rather than establish a democratic nation. During his presidency, the Korean Central Intelligence Agency became a much feared institution and the government frequently imprisoned anyone who opposed them. Park's rule ended on October 26, 1979 when he was killed by his chief of security services.

- Specific planned policies

President Lee Seungman enabled South Korea's first economic spurt, thanks to the implementation of an important land reform. This provided for the redistribution of land, thus removing a potentially problematic social issue. President Park Junghee also made significant contributions to the welfare of South Korea. South Korea began a strong economic recovery after this point and South Korea eventually became the 11th largest economy in the world with a per capita income exceeding $10,000 per year and more than 70% of its population claiming to be middle class.

Despite ongoing pressure from North Korea, President Park Junghee formulated a Five Year Economic Development Plan to boost the South Korea economy with several goals:

- Developing energy industries (such as coal production and electric power)
- Expanding agricultural production and aimed at increasing farm income and correcting the Structural imbalance of the national economy
- Developing basic industries and the economic infrastructure
- Utilizing to the full extent of idle resources; increased employment; conservation and utilization of land

- Improving the balance of payments through export promotion
- Promoting the science and technology

Although this plan did not bring about an immediate self-reliant economy, there was a rapid period of growth out of this policy. The ambitious plan had simply looked for better policies in modernizing and preparing for long-term economic success. The government's efforts were designed to bring about policy reform.

• The New Economy of Korea

Government played the most substantive role in the economic and social development. Korean government launched the first Five-Year Economic Development Plan in 1962 by the political leadership to national development and social stability. During that period, Korean government launched numerous infrastructure development projects with huge amounts of investment such as substantial amount of commercial and concessional loan, and new technology from abroad. And leading producer of ships, steel, automobiles, and semiconductors since 1960s became the major actor of Korean economy.

Following decades of sustained economic growth, Korea became a member of the OECD in 1996 and a decade later, applied to become a member of the OECD-DAC. Upon Korea's request, in 2008 the DAC conducted a review of Korea's development cooperation, with a view toward Korea attaining DAC membership. This review provided Korea with a set of recommendations intended to improve several aspects of its development cooperation system, including the creation of specific legislation to govern its Official Development Assistance (ODA), adjusting its aid architecture, formally and publically committing to ODA targets and grants and loans into one, clear country-level strategy, among others.

In June 2009, the DAC visited Korea to verify whether its development cooperation programme met DAC standards and, on 25 November, the DAC welcomed Korea as a new member.

2. The Korean ODA

Since the 1960s, South Korea has transformed from a recipient country of official development assistance to a significant donor. In 2010, South Korea became a Development Assistance Committee (DAC) member.

• Korea as a recipient country

During the 1950s-1960s, Korea received ODA from foreign countries, a total amount of $12 billion. Especially, right after the Korean War, most of the aid was focused on military support and humanitarian relief. However, in 1960s, 'Growth and foreign investment' replaced "humanitarian relief". And "reconstruction" transformed the Korean economic structure. At the same time, form of aid changed from grants (1950s) to concessional loans (1960s). And during that period, to facilitate reconstruction, Korea government built social infrastructure and promoted industrial development.

There was noticeable change in 1970s-1980s. During this period, Korean government projected financing for the heavy and chemical industries. And in terms of ODA, sector-wide loans or readjustment programmed loans aimed to reform of industries. In 1990s, there was declining in proportion of grants, and sources of assistance was diversified. At the same time in 1990s, Korea was ready to be reverse position from being a recipient to a donor. Korea ended its dependence on the World Bank's assistance in 1995 and was excluded from the DAC list of ODA recipients in 2000.

• History of the Korean ODA

In response to the international community's attention to Korea's successful economic development, Korea started a training program under the sponsorship of the USAID in 1963. Through these programs, the Korean government invited citizens of developing countries to Korea and provided them with training, thereby developing human resources and boosting capacity building in their home countries. In 1965, the Korean government ceased using USAID funds and began paying for these projects with Korea's own budget. Since then, Korea has focused on technical cooperation programs by continuing to host training programs and by dispatching experts and medical staff to its partner countries.

Until the mid-1970s, Korea implemented development assistance mainly funded by the UN. However, the Korean government gradually expanded assistance with its own fund as there was an increasing demand from developing countries pursuing Korea's economic developing path. The Ministry of Foreign Affairs and Trade (MOFAT) procured a budget of \900 million for the first time in 1977 and provided developing countries with equipments and resources. By 1975, Korea's economy had grown to such an extent that Korea no longer qualified for soft loans. Soft loans have the eligibility threshold of $520 per capita income and offer lower interest rates than IBRD development loans to poverty stricken developing countries. In recognition of this amazing growth, the IDA removed Korea from its list of aid recipient countries. In the 1980s, the Korea government was planning for the eventual overseas expansion of its domestic companies and creating a foundation for future business in exports. As early as the 1980s, the Korean government designed a program for the purpose of sharing its experiences of rapid and dynamic development based on the spirit of South-South cooperation. Many believed that Korea's first-hand experiences could be of great help in assisting other developing nations.

In 1982, the Korean Development Institute started the International Development Exchange Program (IDEP) which invited leading figures from developing countries to deliver education programs on Korea's development experience. In 1984, the Ministry of Construction and Transportation (MOCT) and the Ministry of Labor (MOL) launched a project for providing technical assistance in construction and a project for the establishment of a training center respectively. By the time when the Asian Games opened in 1986 and the Seoul Olympics in 1988, Korea accelerated its development assistance as it recorded surplus in the balance of international payments. Korea was also asked to meet responsibility corresponding to its expanded economic capacity and higher status in the international community.

And during the 1980s, Korea's ODA programmes were conducted separately by individual ministries. Due to the increasing number of projects, consolidation was necessary to coordinate projects and make aid more effective. In 1987, EDCF was established to support concessionary loans to developing countries through KEXIM. Through this fund for loan-type aid, Korea set up a base to assist developing countries' industrial and economic development. Also, in 1991, KOICA was founded as an agency responsible exclusively for grant aid under the Ministry of Foreign Affairs and Trade and started providing full-scale assistance for developing countries.

Korea became completely independent of ODA in 1995 when

it stopped receiving loans from the World Bank. Korea's graduation from the World Bank lending list marked the de facto end of Korea's history as a recipient country. Because of this newly found financial independence, Korea was able to become an OECD member country in 1996. Although Korea did receive an emergency financial aid package from international development banks during the Asian financial crisis in 1997, Korea managed to overcome the crisis and in 2000 made its way out of the OECD/DAC list of aid recipients. As such, Korea was finally able to make a transition from an aid-receiving country to an emerging aid-donor country.

In 2007, the Korean government created a team to manage the country's preparation for entering the OECD/DAC. In November 2009, the admission was confirmed and Korea became a new member of the OECD/DAC on 1 January 2010. In January 2010, the Korean government passed the Framework Act on International Development Cooperation, a comprehensive law on ODA. This legislation more clearly articulated ODA goals and basic norms, specified an actual system to combat ODA implementation inefficiencies and fragmentation, and presented a consistent ODA policy.

From 29 November to 1 December 2011, Korea held the fourth High Level Forum on Aid Effectiveness in Busan. Its role and contributions as the host country were widely acknowledged. Among post–World War II independent countries, Korea is the only country to have transformed from an aid recipient to a donor, demonstrating that aid does indeed have a positive effect. With its own development experience of using aid successfully as part of its development and modernization, Korea led the promotion of the "from aid to development" paradigm shift and also helped to achieve agreement on "differential commitments." With the United States, It played leading roles in the inclusion of gender empowerment in the Busan outcome document and acted as a bridge between emerging and traditional donors.

• Goals and Directions of the Korean ODA

Basically Korean ODA has three Goals. First, ODA is assistance for the sustainable socio-economic development of developing countries. Second, Korea ODA pursues the active participation in alleviating poverty through the achievement of the MDGs/SDGs. Third, through the ODA, promotion of humanitarian assistance and human security. And for achieving the goals, Korea established future plans. According to its plan, Korea tries to expand the development cooperation by scaling up its ODA to a level commensurate with its economic standing. Korea tries to achieve the MDGs and address today's global challenges. Last, Korea participates in the global trend of increasing the proportion of grant aid to LDCs (Least Developed Countries).

Under such goals and plans, Korean government set a basic

direction of Korean ODA. Most of all, Korean government will increase the volume of ODA and the ratio of grant aid. Korean government tries to implement a result-based management system that meets the needs of partner countries. Moreover, Korea tries to integrate Korea's development experience and comparative advantages into development cooperation projects/programmes. Also to encourage CSOs (Civil Society Organizations) and the private sector to join Korean programmes. Such directions based on the 'selection and focus' principle. Under such principle the Korean government plans to expand the untied aid and strengthen the capacity for ODA implementation.

3. The Structure of the Korean ODA

• The Committee for International Development Cooperation (CIDC)

The Committee for International Development Cooperation (CIDC) is a coordinating body for deliberating and deciding overall ODA policies for greater policy coherence and systematic delivery of aid programmes. The CIDC composed of 25 members including the Prime Minister, Ministers of related ministries, heads of ODA implementing agencies, and civilian experts. And CIDC hosts the meetings approximately three

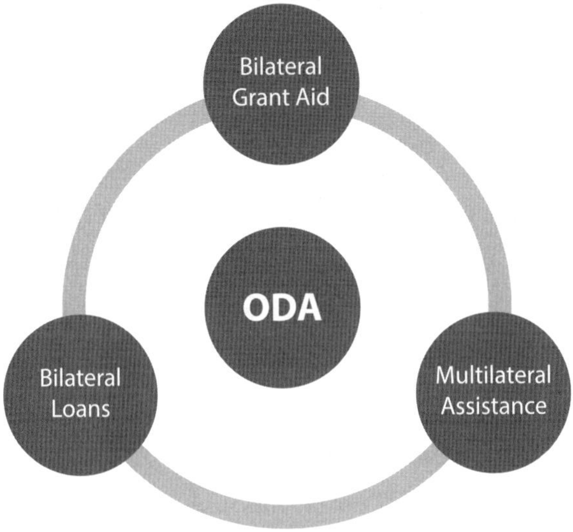

times a year.

And there are also other bodies such as the Working Committee, MOFA and MOSF. The Working committee discusses the agenda in advance of the CIDC meeting and pre-coordinates the policies among the CIDC's 25 members. The Ministry of Foreign Affairs (MOFA) supervises bilateral grant aid, multilateral aid to the UN and other multilateral organizations. The Ministry of Strategy and Finance (MOSF) supervises concessional loans in bilateral aid and cooperation with Multilateral Development Banks (MDBs) in multilateral aid.

• **Bilateral ODA**

Bilateral grant aid includes technical cooperation and various types of transfers made in cash, goods, or services with no obligation for repayment. Such bilateral grant aid is rounds about 40% of the total budget of Korea's bilateral ODA. Bilateral grant aid is conducted by information on the needs and demands of partner countries through policy dialogues and/or demand surveys. The main authorities are Korea International Cooperation Agency (KOICA) and Ministry of Foreign Affairs (MOFA).

Another form of bilateral ODA is bilateral Loans. Bilateral loans provided on concessional terms under the name of the Economic Development Cooperation Fund (EDCF) since 1987. Such bilateral loans are repayments and interests for long time. The main authorities are Korea Export-Import Bank (Korea Eximbank) and Ministry of Strategy and Finance (MOSF).

From 1990 to 2009, 63.6% of Korea's bilateral ODA was allocated to the Asian region and 13% was given to African nations, making the African region Korea's second largest regional recipient. Latin America came next, receiving 7.8% of Korea's bilateral ODA, followed by Europe at 3.9%, and Oceania at 0.8%. In the last 20 years, the country that received the largest amount of aid was Iraq, followed by Vietnam and Indonesia. The Korean government delivered a meager $ 630,000 of assistance to Iraq from 1990 to 2002, but this figure greatly increased after the war in 2003 as Korea assisted with postwar reconstruction and peace building. From 1990 to 2009, fourteen of Korea's top twenty aid recipients were Asian countries; only six aid recipient countries, including Angola and Ghana, were in other regions.

Over the last 20 years, the vast majority of Korea's bilateral ODA has been spent on improving social infrastructure (45%) and economic infrastructure (39%). The small remaining portion was divided between the manufacturing sector (6.2%), emergency relief (2.5%), and other industries (2.2%). ODA for the economic infrastructure and service sector experienced steady modest increase up to 2005, but has been rapidly increasing since 2006.

• Multilateral Assistance

Multilateral assistance indicates the financial subscriptions or (grant) contributions to international organizations. Such multilateral assistance runs or supports (multilateral) international activities and is divided by two sections (subscriptions and contributions). In the case of Korea, main authorities of multilateral assistance are Ministry of Foreign Affairs, Ministry of Strategy and Finance. The Ministry of Foreign Affairs contributes to international organizations. The Ministry of Strategy and Finance subscribes to international organizations. There are many types of international organizations such as the OECD, UN, UNDP, MDBs.

The volume of Korea's multilateral ODA increased from $48.9 million in 1990 to $230 million in 2009. This increase seems dramatic, however, it must be taken into account that a majority of this ODA was in the form of contributions to MDBs and contributions to other organizations. Korea's multilateral ODA consists of contributions to UN organizations and MDBs including the World Bank and regional development banks, other international organizations, and non-governmental organizations. In terms of contribution by organization, the World Bank and regional development banks received 38.5% and 30.8% respectively from 1990 to 2009, accounting for about 70% of multilateral ODA. Contributions to UN organizations accounted for 23.1%.

Lecture 9. Korean ODA in the International Society

1. Korea in the Governing Bodies of the UN
2. UNESCO in Korea
3. Korea in the OECD System
4. The Korean Works in the WTO and the ADB
5. Other Korean ODA Activities

Korean ODA in the International Society

1. Korea in the Governing Bodies of the UN

• The activities of Korea in the ECOSOC

The Economic and Social Council (ECOSOC) is at the heart of the United Nations system to advance the three dimensions of sustainable development–economic, social and environmental. It is the central platform for fostering debate and innovative thinking, forging consensus on ways forward, and coordinating efforts to achieve internationally agreed goals. It is also responsible for the follow-up to major UN conferences and summits. The UN Charter established ECOSOC in 1945 as one of the six main organs of the United Nations. Activities of Korea in the ECOSOC are detailed in below table.

Korea for the ECOSOC

- 1993~1995, 1997~1999, 2003~2006, 2008~2010

Functional Commissions of ECOSOC

- Commission on Narcotic Drugs (CND) 1963~1968, 1982~1985, 1992~2003, 2006~2009
- Commission on Population and Development (CPD) 1996~2001
- Commission on Sustainable Development (CSD) 1993~1995, 1999~2006, 2007~2010
- Commission on the Status of Women (CSW) 1994~2001, 2002~2006, 2006~2010
- Statistical Commission 2004~2007
- Commission for Social Development (CSocD) 1996~2008, 2008~2012
- Commission on Crime Prevention and Criminal Justice (CCPCJ) 2003~2005, 2006~2008, 2009~2011
- Commission on Science and Technology for Development (CSTD) 1998~2001

Subsidiary Organ of ECOSOC

- Commission for Programs and Coordination (CPC) 1993~2007, 2008~2010

• **Korea in the Governing Bodies**

Other UN bodies are also related to the Korean ODA works. Main activities of Korea in other UN bodies are detailed in below table.

Governing Bodies for Funds and Programes in UN

- UN Children's Fund (UNICEF) 1988~1997, 2006~2008, 2009~2011
  UNDP/UNFPA Executive Board 1994~1995, 1998~2000, 2008~2010
- UN Environmental Programs (UNEP) 1987~1989, 1994~2005, 2006~2009
- UN Human Settlements Programs (UN-HABITAT) 1997~2000, 2009~2012

Governing Bodies of the Special Agencies for International Development and Cooperation in UN

- UNESCO 1987~2003, 2007~2011
- International Labor Organization (ILO) 1996~2009, 2008~2011
- Food and Agriculture Organization(FAO) 1965~1967, 1989~2006, 2007~2009
- International Fund for Agricultural Development (IFAD) 2008~2011
- UN Industrial Development Organization (UNIDO)

1995~2003

- Industrial Development Board 2007-2011
- World Health Organization (WHO) 1960~1963, 1984~1987, 1995~1998, 2001~2004, 2007~2010

2. UNESCO in Korea

• Korea and UNESCO

Korea is 55th member of UNESCO (14 June 1950). Korea contributes to UNESCO through increasing regular and voluntary contributions to UNESCO's budget, and by sponsoring UNESCO Prizes. Korea also participates in UNESCO's policy-making process including the UNESCO General Conference and the Executive Board, the governing bodies of inter-governmental committees and institutions and Sub-regional and regional consultation meetings. Korea is a permanent delegate to UNESCO, contributing $ 3,172,927 which takes up to 2.260% of the organization, and there are also UNESCO funds in trust by Korea. The 'Education for All' is under the Ministry of Education and Human Resources Development. East Asian Biosphere Reserve Network is under the Ministry of Environment. And Cultural Heritage of Koguryo Kingdom in North Korea is under the Cultural Heritage Administration.

- **Korea National Commission for UNESCO**

UNESCO is the only organization in UN that has National Commission members. The Korean National Commission for UNESCO was founded (January 1954) in accordance with the UNESCO constitution and a presidential decree. Korea national commission for UNESCO works to further strengthen existing cooperative relationships with its stakeholders at the national, regional, and international levels. Korea national commission for UNESCO pursues the goals of UNESCO in Korea. Such activities are based on the Act on UNESCO Activities (1963). That act provides the Commission with a firm legal basis for carrying out the functions and guides principles for the autonomy of the organization, its finances and program management.

- **The Act on UNESCO Activities (1963)**

The Act on UNESCO Activities is for the UNESCO activities in Korea and covers the Establishment of Korean National Commission for UNESCO. The main purpose of the Act is subscribed in Article 1. According to Article 1, the purpose of Korea National Commission for UNESCO is prescribing matters required for letting Korean Government and people actively participate in the activities of the United Nations Educational, and Scientific and Cultural organization (UNESCO).

The Korea National Commission for UNESCO works in order

to embody the spirit of UN. Therefore, activities of the Commission are pursued by the related international laws such as the UN Charter, the UNESCO Charter, and even the Universal Declaration of Human Rights. The following table displays the structure of related articles.

Chapter 1. General Provisions
Article 1. Purpose
Article 2. Definitions

Chapter 2. UNESCO Activities
Article 3. Objects of UNESCO Activities
Article 4. International Cooperation for UNESCO Activities
Article 5. UNESCO Activities by State and Local Government
Article 6. UNESCO Activities by People

In Article 2, the term 'UNESCO activities' is defined. UNESCO activities are activities to realize the purposes of the UNESCO such as strengthening international cooperation in the competent fields such as education, science and culture, as well as exchange of information and human resources, and as well as the support for researches in the competent fields such as education, science and culture, as well as support for programs and projects. There are many other activities aimed to realize the purposes of UNESCO. Article 3 of the Act provides the objects of UNESCO Activities in Korea as below;

> *"The objects of UNESCO activities in Korea is to enhance mutual understanding and friendship among different countries and cultures, and to diffuse new and diverse cultures and knowledge by facilitating international exchange and cooperation in the competent fields such as education, science and culture, thereby contributing to the establishment of world peace and improvement of welfare for human beings."*

The following table displays the structure of a Korea national committee related articles.

Chapter 3. Korean National Commission for UNESCO
Article 7. Establishment of Korean National Commission for UNESCO
Article 8. Functions and Roles
Article 9. Consultation on Affairs Related to Diplomatic Policy, Etc.
Article 10. Organization of Commission, Etc.
Article 11. Duties of Chairman
Article 12. Term of Office for Members, Etc.
Article 13. Reasons for Disqualification of Members, Etc.
Article 14. Auditor

Article 15. General Assembly

Article 16. Function of General Assembly

Article 17. Operation of General Assembly, Etc.

Article 18. Executive Committee

Article 19. Functions of Executive Committee

Article 20. Subcommittee, Etc

Article 21. Payment of Actual Costs

Article 22. Secretariat

Article 23. Report

Article 24. Operating Regulations

Especially, Article 8 provides the details of the functions and roles of the Commission as below;

- *Stimulation of participation in UNESCO activities by the State, local governments, agencies and organizations in the fields related to UNESCO activities, as well as individuals;*
- *Research and deliberation on matters required for setting up Government policies and concluding international agreements in relation to UNESCO activities, and recommendation and counseling to the heads of central administrative agencies concerned;*
- *Deliberation on preparing agenda to be presented to UNESCO General Assembly, selecting representatives to be dispatched to the said Assembly, etc. and subse-*

quent recommendation to the heads of central administrative agencies concerned;

- *Deliberation on matters concerning domestic implementation of matters resolved in international meetings related to UNESCO activities such as UNESCO General Assembly, and recommendation to the heads of central administrative agencies in relation to their implementation methods;*
- *Cooperation with agencies and organizations at home and abroad related to UNESCO activities, and execution of businesses and activities related to UNESCO, and their coordination;*
- *Management and operation of Korea UNESCO House, and other businesses to provide financial resources required for UNESCO activities; and*
- *Other businesses required to facilitate UNESCO activities.*

In case of chapter IV, it handles with the Asia-Pacific Centre of Education for International Understanding (APEIU). The APEIU related clauses are newly inserted in 2012. Mission of the APEIU is promoting education for international understanding and collaborating with educators and institutions. APEIU provides the services as a center of education, training, research and development in the Asia-Pacific Region. The following table displays the structure of APEIU related articles.

Chapter 4. Asia-Pacific Centre of Education for International Understanding(APEIU)

Article 25. Establishment of the Centre

Article 26. Support

Article 27. Applying correspondingly of the Civil Act

3. Korea in the OECD System

• Korea in the OECD

Korea got OECD membership in 1996 and after then, participated many activitics in the organization. Korea is a member of the discussion forum to share national experience, identify best practices and find solutions to common problems. Regional Centre for Competition in Seoul (2004) is representative case. Regional Centre for Competition in Seoul was established in cooperation with the Korea Fair Trade Commission and the OECD. It deals with works on competition in the Asian region. Most activities are helping the authorities concerned to develop and implement effective competition law and policy.

The OECD Green Growth Strategy Synthesis Report (2011) is Korea's another activity. Such report is for the practical framework for governments to boost economic growth and protect the environment. Through the report, Korea shared its experiences through Korea's Green Growth policies.

• As a member of the DAC

Korea joined the DAC in 2010. In 2010, there was G20 Seoul summit in Korea. During the summit, ODA related issues were handled. For example, the "Seoul Development Consensus for Shared Growth" and "Multi-Year Action Plan on Development" was G20 development agenda. It was tailored for developing countries in key areas toward sustainable and inclusive economic growth.

In 2011, Korea was Co-Chairs of the G20 Development Working Group which was for implementing the G20 development agenda at the Cannes Summit. In same year, there also was the Fourth High Level Forum on Aid Effectiveness (HLF-4) in Korea. It was an opportunity for the international community to forge a new and inclusive global development partnership for more results-oriented and partner country-driven development cooperation

• The International Laws for the Activities of the OECD in Korea

For supporting the activities of the OECD in Korea, the government has established many related international laws. Most representative law is an agreement between the Government of the Republic of Korea, the Organization for Economic Cooperation, Development on the Secondment of Public Officials to the OECD (2007), Memorandum of Understanding between the Government of the Republic of Korea, the Organisation for Economic Cooperation and Development on the Establishment of an OECD/KOREA Policy Centre (2008).

- Agreement between the Government of the Republic of Korea and the Organization for Economic Co-operation and Development on the Secondment of Public Officials to the OECD (2007)

The purpose of this agreement is "desiring to promote mutual co-operation through the secondment of public officials of the Government as project staff (hereinafter referred to as "KPS") who would benefit by gaining experience in international co-operation activities such as those of the OECD, under the close direction of experienced OECD officials, while contributing to the implementation of the programs and activities". The following table shows the structure of agreement.

Contents

Article 1. Recruitment Procedures

Article 2. Status

Article 3. Grade

Article 4. Extension

Article 5. Evaluation

Article 6. Financing Procedures

Article 7. Financing costs

Article 8. Amendments to the Agreement

Article 9. Entry into Force and Duration of this Agreement

Article 10. Dispute Settlement

Article 11. Transitional Measures

- Memorandum of Understanding between the Government of the Republic of Korea and the Organisation for Economic Co-operation and Development on the Establishment of an OECD/KOREA Policy Centre (2008)

The purpose of this memorandum is recalling the four OECD sectoral centers located in Seoul: the Korea-OECD Multilateral Tax Centre, created in 1997; the OECD-Korea Regional Centre for Competition, created in 2003; the Regional Centre on Health and Social Policy, created in 2005; the OECD Asian Centre for Public Governance, created in 2005.

The memorandum considers that the parties agreed on the desirability of merging these four sectoral centers into one single entity located in Seoul, to be identified as the OECD/Korea Policy center. The memorandum also considers that the budget of the center shall be agreed upon separately by the parties and considers that the basic legal framework for the privileges and immunities of OECD, its staff and experts in Korea is provided by the Agreement between the Government of the Republic of Korea and the OECD on the Privileges and Immunities granted to the organization, done in Paris on 15 April 1996. The following table shows the structure of memorandum.

Contents

Article 1. General Principles
Article 2. Purpose
Article 3. OECD Staff in Paris
Article 4. Local Korean Staff
Article 5. Steering Committee
Article 6. Advisory Board
Article 7. Budget
Article 8. Responsibilities of the Parties

4. The Korean Works in the WTO and the ADB

• The works of Korea for the issue in the WTO

Korea joined in GATT system in 1967 and got membership of WTO in 1995. Both GATT system and WTO are multilateral negotiations in international trade. In international trade field, there are issues which related to development. Especially, Korea has a leading role in the field of "Aid for trade" with the experiences of economic development. Korea donated to finance technical assistance programs for developing and least developed countries as well as economies in transition such as $350,000 to the Doha Development Agenda Global Trust Fund (2011) and $350,000 (2014).

And Korea enhanced the ability to participate effectively in the WTO negotiations and ensure they fully benefit from the results such as trade-related technical assistance activities to help developing and least-developed countries (LDCs) to improve their participation in the Doha Round and better integrate into the world economy.

• "e-Asia and Knowledge Partnership Fund" from Korea in the ADB

The "e-Asia and Knowledge Partnership Fund" was established in June 2006 by Korea. For that fund, $20 million was the basis of the fund and $6.37 million as the additional contribution to the Fund (2010) plus another $6 million (2011). That fund' s main goal is "Creating and sharing of knowledge through information and communications technology (ICT) in the Asia and Pacific region" to bridge the digital divide and promote improved access to information. Through tha t fund, "strengthening the capacity of DMCs to achieve the targets of the World Summit on the Information Society (WSIS) Plan of Action" was launched. Such project provides technical assistance for promoting ICT and bridging the digital divide, through national and regional e-strategies.

5. Other Korean ODA Activities

• CLMV position in Korea's ODA

Cambodia, Laos, Mynmar, and Vietnam–known as CLMV–are one of ASEAN member countries not joined after the formation of ASEAN. They are considered to be countries with the biggest investment advantages because of natural resources and low labor power. However, the CLMV is still considered to be the LDC compared to those of more advanced developing nations such as Indonesia, Thailand, and Malaysia. The gaps between these countries are at a serious level where the width of gap is growing bigger. Korea has been highly focusing its ODA programs towards the CLMV countries.

Cambodia

Cambodia has been the recent focus point of Korea's ODA starting from 2004. Unlike other countries, Korea's ODA program in Cambodia is evenly distributed among the main cores of development: educational development, social and economic infrastructure, and training of industrial workers. To ensure the basic needs of industrial development and other capacities industrial workers and volunteers were sent to Cambodia by the Korean ODA program. In social and economic infrastructure projects Korea has sent volunteers teaching socio-cultural projects such as teaching Taekwondo. Mainly this is because of Cambodia's present political and social stability. Recently KOICA has launched a Korea's Request Survey Workshop to promote better understanding of Korea's development agenda, priorities scheme, and administrative procedures for KOICA grant aid projects and also strengthening development cooperation partnership between the two countries. In 2014 Korea's ODA reached $82 million giving a great impact on Cambodia's development level, even though Cambodia like Vietnam is moving from a lower income country to a lower – middle income country.

Laos

Laos is one of the 10 recipient's countries that receive ODA programs from Korea. With receiving $35 million in 2011, Korea contribution in Laos ODA is distributed primarily to social and economic infrastructure projects assuming more than 40% of the total ODA provided. These are done by providing training for industrial workers and volunteers. Recently Korea is pushing and implementing to double the budget of development assistance to Laos. This reflects the desire to support development in ASEAN regions as well as to influence Korea's influence in Laos and ASEAN.

Myanmar

Myanmar is considered to have one of the lowest income rates in the ASEAN region, however the country has great potential for economic development agendas. Like Laos and Cambodia, ODA towards Myanmar has increased drastically over the decade. Mainly the development agendas were focused on invitation of industrial workers trainee, development studies, volunteers, and economic and social infrastructure projects. Investment towards ODA in Myanmar counts approximately $3.2 billion (provided with private sectors). However recent political and social stability of Myanmar has pushed down ODA programs towards Myanmar, before more development programs can be conducted in Myanmar safer environment of social political stability is needed within the region.

Vietnam

Vietnam has always been the largest recipient of Korea's ODA funds in the CLMV Group. Reaching almost 14% of the total budget of ODA in 2011, Vietnam is ranked number one in receiving development assistance from Korea. Overall Korea is expected to raise its development budget to $1.2 billion until 2015 where most of the budget will be focused on funding green growth, improving infrastructure system and human resource development. These priorities are expected to help Vietnam become a more modern industrial country until the 2020. Vietnam is still the largest recipients from Korea though it is becoming a middle income country with rapid growing economy over the past few years. Vietnam still needs a large amount of capital in further to develop mainly its infrastructure development. Korea has devised its ODA program for Vietnam to achieve sustainable development growth, improve infrastructure, and developing rural areas contrasting with Korea's earlier developing agendas that were aimed at social benefits such as health, education, and employment.

• Country Partnership Strategy (CPS) for Central Asian Countries: Kazakhstan, Uzbekistan and Azerbaijan

Korea prepares CPS for the countries selected as priority partner countries, and CPS for Kazakhstan and Uzbekistan of CIS countries could be found in 'Country Assistance Strategy 2009-2011' that Ministry of Foreign Affairs and Trade prepared for grant aid priority partner countries in 2008. Also, CPS for Azerbaijan was released to public recently in 2012.

CAS for Kazakhstan

Korean government's assistance strategy for Kazakhstan is basically based on Kazakhstan development strategy, its major goal is to support and realize it, and it is stated that the direction of support is to find and promote towards administration and development capability reinforcement, teaching development experience of Korea rather than equipment support if possible. Especially, its core is to contribute to expand cooperation between two countries in the mid and long term by the support of economic development planning in which trials and errors could be experienced by Kazakhstan for the fast economic development process and reinforcement of cooperation in human resource development, ICT, and health and medical industry in which Korean has comparative advantage based on development experience of Korea.

To specifically analyze 3 main goals shown in Kazakhstan's CAS, Korea concentrates on the following sectors, considering Kazakhstan development plan and comparative advantage of Korea to support the strategies for entry to the 50 greatest competitiveness nations that Kazakhstan government promotes: 1) establishment of sustainable economic development framework, 2) economic structure improvement for economic development acceleration, 3) education and training reinforcement and vulnerable group protection. In addition, the following priority support sectors are selected considering specific strategies to perform of entry strategy to 50 greatest competitiveness nations Kazakhstan government promotes: 1) sustainable economic development, 2) economic innovation, 3) modern welfare policy promotion, and comparative advantage Korea.

CAS for Uzbekistan

Korea set up the following 3 main goals while considering welfare promotion of poverty group with placing priority on Uzbek government's economic development capability reinforcement, based on the fact that WIS promotes poverty eradication and MDGs goal accomplishment through persistent high rate economic growth and distribution, and social safety network establishment: 1) qualitative level improvement of public sector' s capability reinforcement project, 2) active support of private sector's development, 3) efforts to improve poverty group's welfare. Uzbekistan is a base country in Central Asia, abundant in natural resources with great cooperative potential with us, and Uzbekistan plans to persistently expand aid scale in the future because she values the promotion of cooperation relation with us under the strategic judgment that our experience of economic development would be a model of her economic development.

Accordingly, Korea plans to find and promote project of comparative advantage in accordance with 'selection and concentration principle' such as discovery of project for our unique development experience to be applicable for and provision of goal centered and performance oriented aid. It was found that the priority support sector for Uzbekistan is concentrated mostly on the support of education, health, ICT, and administration system sector. Especially, the support is concentrated specialized profession education in the education sector, emergency medical service improvement in the health and medical sector, administration capability reinforcement of government in the administration system sector, and concentrated on electronic government establishment in the ICT sector, which is similar to in Kazakhstan.

CPS for Azerbaijan

CPS for Azerbaijan has set the intense cooperation fields for: Strengthening the basis of economic development in non-petroleum fiends through water resource development and stable power supply, and Striving for the sustainable development through improvement of public sector system and productivity improvement. From the detailed promotion plan of the water resource development of Azerbaijan's SPSEDR 2009-2013, Korea plans to support in structuring of water resource development system in some subject area, establishment of mid- to long-term development and investment plan for water resource, strengthen operation competency, disposition of water and sewer system and the like to contribute to securing of stable water supply and improvement of environment.

Through structuring of recycled energy development system in hydraulic power, wind power, solar energy and the like, system improvement, cooperation in energy efficiency technology, competency in pertinent manpower, it also plans to strengthen energy efficiency increase and industrial base for each field. In the meantime, it plans to support architecture for each field of government, people and business as well as structuring of online service system in public sector to improve efficiency and transparency of administrative affairs as well as strengthen the administration with participation of general public, and it also plans to support the technical cooperation for economic facilitation strategy for each field and preparation of system improvement plan, advancement of human resource capability in public administration to enhance productivity, and advancement of ICT specialized human resources.

Lecture 10. International Law for the Korean ODA Works

1. The Mainstream of the International Law for the ODA Works in Korea

2. The Laws for Korea ODA
(International Agreements for the Recipient)

3. The Laws for Korean ODA Works

International Law for the Korean ODA Works

1. The Mainstream of the International Law for the ODA works in Korea

Among post–World War independent countries, Korea is the only country to have transformed from an aid recipient to a donor country, demonstrating that aid does indeed have a positive effect.

In 1970s, most agreements for Korean ODA works are about grants and loans to Korea as a recipient. In reality, after the World War II, in the geopolitical context of the Cold War, Korea in the 1950s received emergency relief as well as reconstruction funds from the international community. During the period of 1945-1953, ODA projects in Korea focused mainly on post war rehabilitation and during 1953-1960, the aid was focused on the reconstruction. In 1961, the focus of the ODA to Korea changed to supporting economic independence.

However, various agreements for Korean ODA works nowadays are based on aid or international cooperation from Korea to developing countries as a donor, such as making fund, dispatching expert and establishing a policy centre in Korea. With the economic development, Korea became an Organization for Economic Cooperation and Development (OECD) member in 1996. Although Korea did receive an emergency financial aid package from international development banks during the Asian financial crisis in 1997, they made its way out of the OECD list of aid recipients in 2000. The country showed the successful economic development to make the transition from an aid-receiving country to an emerging aid-donor country."

2. The Laws for Korea ODA (International Agreements for the Recipient)

In 1950s-1980s (mainly 1970s), most of laws are for the poverty reduction projects after the Korean War and for the Economic development project of the Korean government. International Rules (or Methods) are bilateral agreements between Korea and a certain donor state, bilateral agreements between Korea and a certain International institution (such as the World Bank group and Agencies in the UN), and multilateral agreements for special funds and building organizations. There are several examples of the laws as below;

- **Loan Agreement between the Republic of Korea and International Bank for Reconstruction and Development** (1970)

The purpose of the agreement is to confirm the finance from the IBRD for the Korean (railway) infrastructure reconstruction work. The main framework of the agreement is as below;

Article 1. General Conditions; Definitions
Article 2 . The Loan
Article 3. Use of the Proceeds Loan
Article 4. Bonds
Article 5. Particular Covenants
Article 6. Remedies of the Bank
Article 7. Effective Date; Termination
Article 8. Miscellaneous
Schedule 1. Amortization Schedule
Schedule 2. Premiums on Prepayment and Redemption

According to the Section 2.01 of Article II, the Bank (IBRD) agrees to lend $4 million to the Borrower (the Korean government) on the terms and conditions in this Loan Agreement set forth. Then, the Borrower shall pay interest at the rate of 7% per year on the principal amount of the Loan withdrawn and outstanding from time to time (SECTION 2.06).

• Development Credit Agreement between Republic of Korea and International Development Association (1970)

The purpose of this development credit agreement is similar to the former agreement. The Korean government as the Borrower previously requested the IDA and IBRD to assist in the financing of the railway project. With this bilateral law, the Borrower and the Association could agree to establish more financial assistance. The main framework of the agreement is as below;

Article 1. General Conditions: Definitions
Article 2. The credit
Article 3. Use of the Proceeds of the Credit
Article 4. Particular Covenants
Article 5. Remedies of the Association
Article 6. Effective Date; Termination
Article 7. Miscellaneous
Schedule 1. Allocation of the Proceeds of the Credit and of the Loan
Schedule 2. Description of Investment Plan and Project
A. The Investment Plan / B. The Project
Schedule 3. Procurement

According to the Section 2.01, The Association agrees to land $15 million to the Korean government (Borrower) on the terms and conditions in this Agreement set forth.

• Agreement between the Government of the Republic of Korea and the United Nations Development Programme (1987)

This agreement was established based on the Korean government's request of the assistance to the UNDP. The main framework of the agreement is as below;

Article 1. Scope of this Agreement
Article 2. Forms of Assistance
Article 3. Execution of Projects
Article 4. Information concerning Project
Article 5. Participation and Contribution of Government in Execution of Project
Article 6. Assessed Programme Costs and Other Items Payable in Local Currency
Article 7. Relation to Assistance from Other Sources
Article 8. Use of Assistance
Article 9. Privileges and Immunities
Article 10. Facilities for Execution of UNDP Assistance
Article 11. Suspension or Termination of Assistance
Article 12. Settlement of Disputes
Article 13. General Provisions

According to Article 2, the assistance which may be made available by the UNDP to the Korean government under this agreement may consist of:

- The services of advisory experts and consultants, including consul tank firms or organizations, selected in consultation with the Government by any responsible to. the UNDP or the Executing Agency concerned ;

- The services of operational experts selected the Executing Agency, in consultation with the Government, to perform functions of an operational, executive or administrative character as employees of such entities as the Government may designate under Article 1, paragraph 2, hereof;

- The services of members of the United Nations Volunteers (hereinafter called volunteers);

- Equipment and supplies not readily available in the Republic of Korea (hereinafter called the country);

- Seminars, training programmes, demonstration projects, expert working groups and related activities;

- Scholarships and fellowships, or similar arrangements under with candidates nominated by the Government and approved by the Executing Agency concerned may study or receive training; and

- Any other form of assistance which may be agreed upon by the Government and the UNDP

There are many obligations to the recipient. Under this law, Korea shall provide the UNDP with all appropriate facilities band relevant information to appraise the request, including an expression of its intent with respect to the follow-up of investment-oriented projects. Furthermore, Korea shall remain responsible for its UNDP-assisted development projects and realization of their objectives as described in the relevant Project Documents, and shall carry out such parts of such projects as may be stipulated in the provisions of this agreement and such Project Documents.

3. The Laws for Korean ODA Works

• Agreement Concerning the Use of Experts for Technical Cooperation among Developing Counties (1995)

This Agreement was concluded between Korea and the Food and Agriculture Organization (FAO) of the UN. The purpose of the FAO Scheme is to foster technical cooperation among developing countries, on priority programmes in the fields of agriculture, forestry and fisheries, with a view to promoting the individual and collective self-reliance of developing countries through exchange of experience, sharing of technical expertise and development of complementary capacities. The main framework of the agreement is as below;

Article 1. Participation in the Scheme
Article 2. Purpose of the Scheme
Article 3. Project Agreements

Article 4. Obligations of the Releasing Government

Article 5. Obligations of the Beneficiary Government

Article 6. Obligations of FAO

Article 7. Review of Amounts of Monetary Payments

Article 8. Entry into Force

Article 9. Amendments and Termination

According to Article 3, the Korean government will inform FAO in respect of each particular project or series of projects whether it wishes to participate in those projects as a country requesting assistance (Beneficiary Government) or as a country providing expert service (Releasing Government). The particular conditions for expert assignments within the framework of this agreement shall be set out in specific agreements to be concluded for each particular project or series of projects by the Beneficiary Government, the Releasing Government and FAO.

Therefore, Korea as a Releasing Government will select suitable experts meeting the requirements specified by the Beneficiary Government. The Korean government will be responsible for the salary of the experts. The selection of each expert will be subject to the approval of the Beneficiary Government and of FAO. Then, the Beneficiary Government will assume responsibility for the payment of reasonable local expenses of board and lodging for each expert during the period that he is working on an approved project in the country of the Beneficiary Government.

- **Memorandum of Understanding between the Government of Republic of Korea and the United Nations Development Programme concerning the Establishment of a Trust Fund** (1996)

This Memorandum of Understanding (MOU) is for the establishment and the regulation of the special trust fund from the Korean government to the UNDP. According to the rule, the Korean government promised to establish the special fund as a donor. The trust fund under this agreement is utilized to finance projects by the UNDP in consultation with Korea and the recipient countries. The MOU consists of 10 articles for the establishment of the $1 million Trust Fund and the administration of the fund.

- **Partnership Framework Agreement between the Government of the Republic of Korea and the United Nations Development Programme** (2006)

The Korean government and the UNDP established deeper partnership for further co-project works. For the purpose, they agreed to cooperate in the form of co-financing development projects and programs. Under this framework agreement, Korea may make available contributions in the form of grants for the projects to be administered by UNDP. The agreement consists of 11 articles for the purpose. The main framework of the agreement is as below;

Article 1. Competent Authority

Article 2. Selection of Projects

Article 3. Co-Financing Commitment and Acceptance

Article 4. Procurement

Article 5. Deposit and Disbursement of Contributions

Article 6. Cooperation and Consultation

Article 7. Administrative Cost Recovery

Article 8. Communications

Article 9. Miscellaneous

According to Article 2, the Korean government (MOFA) shall indicate to UNDP the countries and sectors that it considers of particular priority for co-financing with UNDP in accordance with the Korean development policy. The UNDP shall periodically provide MOFA with a list of Projects which UNDP is assisting or intends to assist and which have a potential for co-financing with MOFA. Then, each project to be co-financed under this Agreement shall be selected by the Korean government in consultation with UNDP and the relevant recipient.

Article 3 provides the regulations of the co-financing commitment. Korea will contribute funds to UNDP under this Agreement to finance the costs of Project activities. All of the co-financing to be provided under this Agreement shall be provided on a grant basis. Then, UNDP shall be responsible for the administration of an arrangement established under this Agreement. In this case, Korea may request consultations regarding the administration of such arrangement in accordance with Article 6 of this Agreement.

- **Agreement for the Establishment of the KOREA-UNDP MDG Trust Fund between the Government of the Republic of Korea and the United Nations Development Programme (2009)**

This agreement is for another cooperation work between Korea and the UNDP. The two parties considered the critical importance of a strong partnership of all development actors to achieve the MDG and they decided to establish a special trust fund for the achievement of the goal. The Korean government and the UNDP decided to enter into this Agreement in order to further strengthen their cooperation and partnership through the establishment of a Korea-UNDP MDG Trust Fund for programmatic, fund-based cooperation starting from the year 2010, under the Financial Regulations and Rules of UNDP. The main framework of the agreement is as below;

Article 1. Purpose
Article 2. Contribution
Article 3. Management of the Fund
Article 4. Administrative and Support Services
Article 5. Equipment
Article 6. Audit
Article 7. Reporting

Article 8. Monitoring and Evaluation

Article 9. Visibility

Article 10. Addresses/Communication

Article 11. Other Matters

Article 12. Settlement of Disputes

Article 13. Amendment

Article 14. Entry into Force and Termination

According to Article 2, the Trust Fund shall be financed from contributions by the Korean government on an annual basis. The Korean government shall inform the UNDP of the amount of its annual contribution prior to the start of each new fiscal year. Then, the financial resources contributed to the Fund will be managed by the UNDP in accordance with its Financial Regulations and Rules, policies and procedures. Furthermore, the UNDP shall manage the Fund in accordance with UNDP Financial Regulations and Rules, policies and procedures.

Article 3 provides the details on the management of the fund. For the purpose, they agreed to build a Steering Committee comprised of the representatives of the Korean government and the UNDP. The committee is constituted to make all final decisions regarding the activities to be financed based on the consensus. However, the identification, preparation, appraisal and supervision of the programmes or projects under this Fund will be the sole responsibility of UNDP, and will be carried out by UNDP in accordance with UNDP's Financial Regulations and

Rules, policies and procedures.

- **Agreement between the Government of the Republic of Korea And the United Nations Development Programme Relating to the Establishment Of the UNDP Seoul Policy Centre for Global Development Partnerships (2010)**

The partnership between the Korean government and the UNDP has evolved over time with the conclusion of the Partnership Framework Agreement in 2006 and the establishment of the MDG Trust Fund in 2010. Then, the partners were also interested in establishing a Policy Center on Global Development Partnerships. The agreement consists of 21 articles and the main framework of the articles is as below;

Article 1. Establishment and Location
Article 2. Functions and Activities of the Policy Center
Article 3. Legal Capacity
Article 4. Applicability of the Convention to the Policy Center
Article 5. Policy Center Personnel
Article 6. Financing
Article 7. Premises and Security
Article 8. Public Services
Article 9. Communications and Publications
Article 10. Archives

Article 11. Funds, Assets and Other Property

Article 12. Exemption from Taxation

Article 13. Participants in the Policy Center's Meetings

Article 14. Flag and Emblem

Article 15. Access, Transit and Residence

Article 16. Identification

Article 17. Privileges and Immunities

Article 18. Laissez-Passer

Article 19. Settlement of Disputes

Article 20. Respect for Local Laws and Regulations

Article 21. General Provisions

According to Article 2 of this agreement, the functions and activities of the Policy Center are 1) to serve as the immediate interface with the Government on all aspects relating to the evolving Republic of Korea-UNDP partnership, 2) to serve as a knowledge center for comparative experiences and approaches of new development partners in reducing poverty and achieving sustainable human development, and 3) to facilitate and promote learning, networking, policy dialogue and consultation among new development partners and to contribute to capacity development in developing countries.

The Korean government and the UNDP also agreed to grant the UNDP all the necessary privileges, immunities, and facilities to enable the Policy Center to perform its functions. Article 17 is the main provisions on this regulation. Furthermore, Article 12 provides the issue of the exemption from the national taxation by the Korean government.

Lecture 11. Domestic Laws for the Korean ODA

1. The Main Structure of the Korean ODA Laws
2. Framework Act on International Development Cooperation (2010)
3. KOICA Act and EDCF Act
4. Other Domestic Laws on the Korean ODA Activities

Domestic Laws for the Korean ODA

1. The Main Structure of the Korean ODA Laws

• The CIDC with the Framework Act on International Development Cooperation

The Committee for International Development Cooperation (CIDC), as a coordinating body with the Chair of the Prime Minister, deliberates overall ODA policies for greater policy coherence and systematic delivery of the Korean aid works. The CIDC, based on the Framework Act on International Development Cooperation (Article 7.2), composed of 25 members including the Prime Minister, Ministers of related ministries, heads of ODA implementing agencies, and civilian experts is held approximately three times a year. The CIDC decides upon the framework plans and annual comprehensive implementation plans. It also evaluates the ODA policies and the progress of ODA projects based on the Framework Act. The decisions adopted by the CIDC are legally-binding and monitored every six months. Paragraph 1 of Article 7 in the Framework Act provides the existence of the CIDC as below;

> *"The Committee for International Development Cooperation shall be established under the control of the Prime Minister to deliberate on and moderate major matters to ensure that polices on international development cooperation are implemented in a comprehensive and systematic manner."*

The Working Committee discusses the agenda in advance of the CIDC meeting, and pre-coordinates the policies among its 25 members, which include the Vice Minister of the Prime Minister Office as the chair along with director-level senior officials in relevant ministries and civilian experts. The Sub-Committee for Evaluation deliberates on the evaluation items prior to the CIDC meeting. This Sub-Committee is composed of senior-level officials of the MOSF and MOFA, executives of EDCF and KOICA, and civilian experts. The Sub-Committee for Evaluation appoints 9 civilian experts among 15 committee members in order to ensure professional expertise in evaluation. In addition, the Sub-Committee for Evaluation itself sometimes conducts evaluation on urgent items in need of improvement for the integrated implementation of ODA, and deliberates and approves evaluation results of ODA conducted by implementation agencies. The decisions of the Sub-Committee for the evaluation can be adopted as ODA policies through the discussion of the Working Committee and the CIDC.

Under the Framework Act and other related laws, the Ministry of Foreign Affairs (MOFA) supervises bilateral grant aid and multilateral aid to the UN and other multilateral organizations. The Ministry of Strategy and Finance (MOSF) supervises concessional loans in bilateral aid and cooperation with MDBs in multilateral aid. KOICA is responsible for the bilateral grant aid and technical cooperation programmes under the Ministry of Foreign Affairs (MOFA). Korea Eximbank is responsible for the EDCF loans under the Ministry of Strategy and Finance (MOSF). MOFA and MOSF are responsible for the multilateral assistance; Financial subscriptions (MOSF), Contributions (MOFA).

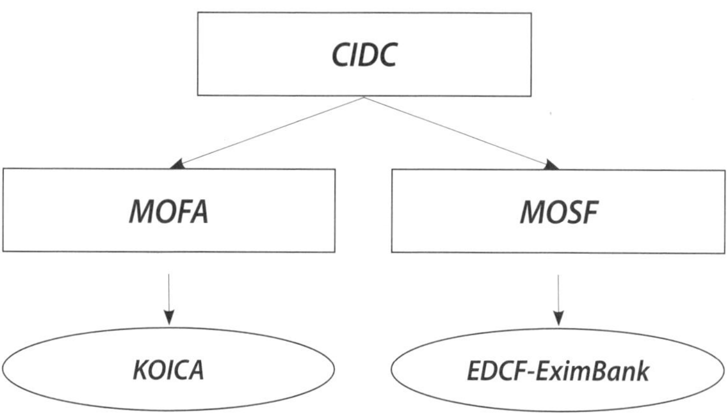

<The structure of the Korean ODA system>

• **Other related laws**

Along with Framework Act and CIDC, there are several laws related to specific ODA agencies and activities. To introduce major regulations;

> Act on the Measures for the Admission to International Financial Institutions (enacted in 1963) regulates the membership with the international financial institutions and measures to discharge the responsibilities as a member prescribed in the agreements governing the respective international financial institutions
>
> Economic Development Cooperation Fund Act (enacted in 1987) regulates the establishment, operation and management of the Economic Development Cooperation Fund as concessional loan
>
> Korea International Cooperation Agency Act (enacted in 1991) sets out the foundation of Korea International Cooperation Agency (KOICA) and its mandates to carry out grant aid projects and technical cooperation
>
> Overseas Emergency Relief Act (enacted in 2007) prescribes the matters necessary for overseas emergency relief, such as dispatch of emergency relief teams, provi-

sion of emergency relief supplies, support for interim recovery from disasters, etc.

2. Framework Act on International Development Cooperation (2010)

• The main structure of the articles

The Framework Act on International Development Cooperation and the Presidential Decree establishes the legal networks with other Korean domestic laws on the aid fields. Therefore, the main purpose of the law is to provide fundamental rules concerning the Korean international development cooperation works including the ODA activities. The articles of the law are also related to the basic system for enhancing appropriateness of international development cooperation policy and efficiency of execution and achieving objective of international development cooperation effectively. The articles of the Framework Act also provide the authorities, the powers, the roles and even evaluation methods. The main structure of the articles as below;

Article 1. Purpose
Article 2. Definitions
Article 3. Basic Ideology and Objectives
Article 4. Basic Principles

Article 5. Obligations of State, etc.

Article 6. Relations with other Acts

Article 7. Committee for International Development Cooperation

Article 8. Formulation, etc. of Basic Plans on International Development Cooperation

Article 9. Agency Supervising International Development Cooperation

Article 10. Roles and Functions of Agency Supervising International Development Cooperation

Article 11. Formulation, etc. of annual Implementation Plans on International Development Cooperation

Article 12. Selection of Priority Cooperation Partners

Article 13. Evaluation of International Development Cooperation

Article 14. Support for Civil International Development Cooperation Organizations, etc.

Article 15. Public Relations, etc. for National Participation

Article 16. Training Specialized Human Resources

Article 17. Strengthening International Exchanges and Cooperation

Article 18. Statistics on International Development Cooperation

Article 19. Roles of Diplomatic Establishments Abroad

Article 20. Entrustment or Delegation of Authority

- **Purpose and main directions**

According to the Article 1, the main purpose of the Framework Act is as below;

> *"The purpose of this Act is to enhance the appropriateness of policies for international development cooperation and the effectiveness of implementation thereof, and effectively achieve the policy objectives of international development cooperation by providing for basic matters concerning international development cooperation, thus contributing to the co-prosperity of humanity and to world peace."*

Article 3 of the Framework Act identifies the five basic directions or ideologies of the Korea's international development cooperation: 1) reduce poverty in developing countries; 2) improve the human rights of women and children, and achieve gender equality; 3) realize sustainable development and humanitarianism; 4) promote cooperative economic relations with developing partners; and 5) pursue peace and prosperity in the international community.

Under these five directions, objectives of the Korea's International Development Cooperation are to achieve the following matters: 1) alleviate poverty and improve the quality of life of people in developing countries; 2) support partner country's development and improve the system and conditions for such development; 3) reinforce friendly relations with developing countries; 4) contribute toward the resolution of global problems related to international development cooperation; and 5) other matters deemed necessary for realizing the basic principles. These visions are reflected in ODA policies and strategies and also repeatedly commented in various global fora on international development cooperation.

As a responsible member of the global community, Korea respects and complies with the international development cooperation standards to strengthen its global partnerships and plans to contribute more to multilateral organizations. To meet this end, Korea sets three major measures implementing multilateral ODA more strategically, complying with global norms and participating in the standard-setting process, and actively participating in global discussions of the international community. Article 4 on Basic Principles provides this regulation as below;

- The State, local governments and other implementing agencies (referred to as the "State, etc." hereinafter) shall conduct projects for international development cooperation by comprehensively considering the following principles and the foreign policy of the Republic of Korea:
  - · Respect for all the principles of the Charter of the United Nations;

· Support for the self-help efforts and abilities of co-operation partners;
· Respect for the necessity for development by cooperation partners;
· Increased sharing of development experiences;
· Promotion of the harmonious relations and cooperation with the international community.

- The State, etc. shall endeavor to strengthen the connection between bilateral development cooperation and multilateral development cooperation, as well as the connection between grant aid and loans, and implement policies for international development co-operation in a consistent manner, thereby maximizing the effectiveness of international development cooperation.

Recognizing the importance of public support, it emphasizes inclusive partnership with private sector from information sharing to joint working in ODA implementation. Korea established 'Whole-of-government Strategy for Public Awareness of ODA' at the 6th meeting of the CIDC in December 2009. To follow this up, the CIDC made task force in 2010 and conducted diverse communication activities including 1) introduction of ODA in elementary and middle school text books (since 2010); 2) development of the Korea' ODA brand identity (BI) (August 2011); and 3) launching integrated website of Korean ODA (January

2012). In addition to these communication activities, the Korean government promotes public education and research through KOICA, universities, or research institutions to foster ODA experts and to enhance public awareness of ODA. The government also has promoted collaboration with private sectors, such as NGOs, business, and academia to find more effective delivering methods to contribute partner countries' dynamic and sustainable development.

• The Provisions on the CIDC and other committees in the Framework Act

As mentioned before, CIDC is established to deliberate on and moderate major matters to ensure that polices on international development cooperation are implemented in a comprehensive and systematic manner. As for the members, CIDC is composed of 25 or less members. They are including the Prime Minister (the chairperson), the Minister of Strategy and Finance, the Minister of Foreign Affairs, the Minister of the Office for Government Policy Coordination (executive secretary), the heads of central administrative agencies and the relevant agencies or organizations, and Persons commissioned by the chairperson from among those with profound knowledge and experience. Article 7 on this regulation is below;

Article 7 (Committee for International Development Cooperation)

- The Committee for International Development Cooperation (referred to as the "Committee" hereinafter) shall be established under the control of the Prime Minister to deliberate on and moderate major matters to ensure that polices on international development cooperation are implemented in a comprehensive and systematic manner.
- The Committee shall consist of 25 or less members, including a chairperson and an executive secretary.
- The Prime Minister shall be the chairperson, and members shall be the Minister of Strategy and Finance, the Minister of Foreign Affairs, the Minister of the Office for Government Policy Coordination, the heads of central administrative agencies and the relevant agencies or organizations determined by Presidential Decree, and persons commissioned by the chairperson from among those with profound knowledge and experience.
- The Minister of the Office for Government Policy Coordination shall be an executive secretary, and he/she shall provide necessary support for the performance of the duties of the Committee and operation thereof.
- The Committee shall deliberate on and moderate the following matters:
    · Basic plans for international development coopera-

tion underArticle 8 and the annual comprehensive implementation plans for international development cooperation underArticle 11 (4);

· Matters concerning the evaluation of international development cooperation underArticle 13;

· Matters requiring coordination by the Government from among policies related to international development cooperation;

· Other matters deemed important and referred by the chairperson.

- The working committee of international development cooperation (referred to as the "working committee" hereinafter) shall be established under the control of the Committee to consult in advance on and moderate agenda items referred by the Committee, and handle matters entrusted by the Committee, and the Vice Minister of the Office for Government Policy Coordination shall assume the post of chairperson of the working committee.
- The Committee may establish the civil advisory committee under its control, when necessary.
- Necessary matters concerning the composition and operation of the Committee, the working committee and the civil advisory committee, other than those prescribed under paragraphs (1) through (7), shall be prescribed by Presidential Decree.

The works of The CIDC covers 1) basic plans for international development cooperation and the annual comprehensive implementation plans for international development cooperation, 2) matters concerning the evaluation of international development cooperation, 3) matters requiring coordination by the Government from among policies related to international development cooperation, and 4) other matters deemed important and referred by the chairperson.

Then, how about an establishment of the Working Committee? The Working Committee, under the control of the CIDC, consults in advance on and moderate agenda items referred by the CIDC and handles matters entrusted by the CIDC. At first, chairperson of the Working Committee is dedicated to the Vice Minister of the Office for Government Policy Coordination. And about the establishment of the Civil Advisory Committee, usually it is under the control of the CIDC. For about more details about it, we'll discuss from below.

• The Provisions on the formation of the ODA plans, etc.

Taking into account global discussions on development cooperation and Korea's current status, the Korean government devised the Strategic Plan for International Development Cooperation (Strategic Plan) at the 7th meeting of the Committee for International Development Cooperation (CIDC) in October 2010. The Strategic Plan clarifies its basic framework for Korea' s international development cooperation policy as follows: 1) to take responsibility as a member of the OECD Development Assistance Committee (DAC); 2) to fulfill its commitment of scaling up the ODA volume; 3) to strengthen integrated ODA system in accordance with the Framework Act.

As one of Strategic Plan, Article 8 of the Act mandated the government to formulate the Mid-term ODA Policy, which sets out policy directions and volume of ODA, and mid-term strategies for a period of five years. The Mid-term ODA Policy for 2011-2015 was approved at the 8th meeting of the CIDC (December 2010) to specify action plan to carry out the Strategic Plan for upcoming five years. It includes annual ODA scaling-up target and ODA allocation guidelines by region and by income group. It also has ODA partnership strategy with major stakeholders such as international organization, NGOs, business, academia, and other foreign donor agencies for improve effectiveness and transparency of ODA.

> Article 8 (Formulation, etc. of Basic Plans on International Development Cooperation)
>
> - The agency supervising international development cooperation underArticle 9 (referred to as the "supervising agency" hereinafter) shall prepare basic draft sectoral plans for international development cooperation (referred to as the "basic draft sectoral plans" hereinafter) every five years and submit them to the Committee, after

undergoing review by the working committee.

- The Committee shall integrate basic draft sectoral plans submitted under paragraph (1) and finalize basic plans for international development cooperation encompassing the following matters:
    - · Basic directions of polices for international development cooperation;
    - · Scale for international development cooperation and operating plans;
    - · Mid-term Assistance Strategies for priority cooperation partners underArticle 12.
    - · The transparency improvement plan in the works
- Notwithstanding the provisions of paragraph (2), matters deemed important by the Committee, among basic draft plans, may be finalized by the President after deliberation by the State Council.
- The Committee may revise basic plans (referred to as "basic plans" hereinafter) finalized under paragraphs (2) and (3) after deliberation and moderation by the Committee within five years, when deemed necessary.
- When the Committee finalizes a basic plan or modifies any important matter prescribed by Presidential Decree, it shall report it to the National Assembly without delay.
- The Committee shall convey basic plans to the supervising agency, which, in turn, shall convey matters

falling under the purview of implementing agencies to the relevant implementing agencies and diplomatic and consular missions (referring to the overseas diplomatic and consular missions of the Republic of Korea under the Act on the Establishment of Overseas Diplomatic and Consular Missions of the Republic of Korea; the same shall apply hereinafter).

- Necessary matters concerning the procedures for formulating basic plans and reporting them to the National Assembly, other than those prescribed under paragraphs (1) through (6), shall be prescribed by Presidential Decree.

In addition, based on the Mid-term ODA Policy, Annual Implementation Plans are devised and used since 2011. The total amount of budget set aside for ODA in 2012 reaches 0.15% of Korea's GNI, which is equivalent to about $1.7 billion among which 70% is bilateral ODA and 30% is multilateral ODA. Within bilateral ODA, grants aid occupies 53% and concessional loan accounts for 47%. In terms of geographic distribution, 43% of the total bilateral ODA will go for Asian countries and 14% will be allocated in African countries. By sector, 36% of the budget will go toward developing the economic infrastructure while 35% will be allocated to support social infrastructure in total amount of bilateral ODA. In the meantime, support for NGOs, emergency relief aid, and public-private partnerships also doubled compared to the previous year. The Ministry of Foreign

Affairs and Trade through KOICA and the Ministry of Strategy and Finance through EDCF will execute about 90% of the annual ODA budget while other governmental agencies implement the remaining 10%.

3. KOICA Act and EDCF Act

• Korea International Cooperation Agency (KOICA) Act

The Korea International Cooperation Agency (KOICA) Act (1991) is about the Establishment, Operation and Management of the KOICA. Based on the Act, the Korea International Cooperation Agency (KOICA) was established in 1991 as a governmental agency responsible for grant aid and technical cooperation for developing countries. The Act provides the legal basis and regulation of the KOICA as one of the main agencies for Korean ODA activities. KOICA operates in five types of programs such as projects, training programs, dispatch of volunteers and experts (World Friends Korea (WFK) programme), and overseas emergency relief, partnership with CSOs and multilateral assistance under this Act. For the works, the KOICA has one headquarters in Korea and about 44 resident missions abroad and they are also regulated based on the law.

According to the Article 7 of the Act, their works for developing countries are 1) Invitation of trainees; 2) Dispatch of professional human resources; 3) Dispatch of Korea Overseas Volunteers; 4) Research in development; 5) Disaster relief; and 6) Assistance with goods, funds and facilities. Then, they also work for international cooperation such as 1) Support to international cooperation activities of non-governmental organizations; 2) Cooperation with foreign aid-related organizations and international organizations; 3) Research and study on the formulation of ideologies and policies on international cooperation; and 4) Other projects necessary for the promotion of international cooperation.

• Economic Development Cooperation Fund Act

The Economic Development Cooperation Fund (EDCF) Act (1986) is about the Establishment and Management of the EDCF. According to the Economic Development Cooperation Fund Act, the Korea Eximbank is entrusted with the operation and administration of the EDCF founded in 1987 as a special fund for concessional loan to developing countries. The special fund supports sustainable development of partner countries by providing concessional loans to establish socio-economic infrastructure necessary to stimulate economic development. Furthermore, it actively operates Public-Private Partnership (PPP) type loans and co-financing with MDBs in order to secure financing in response to the recent request from developing partners on large-size infrastructure development projects.

The works of the EDCF can be related to the other domestic laws. Of course, the Framework Act will be related to the EDCF Act. Then, it also is with the Korea Export-Import Bank Act. Article 8 on the requirement for assistance from the Fund provides below;

> *"Assistance from the Fund as set forth in subparagraphs 1 through 4 ofArticle 7 shall be made available only in cases where it is deemed difficult to obtain financial support from the Export-Import Bank of Korea under the Export-Import Bank of Korea Act (hereinafter referred to as the "Export-Import Bank of Korea") or other banks under ordinary terms and conditions."*

As the activities with the fund, Article 7 on the use of fund can provide the regulation. The fund will be used only for the works below;

- Extending loans (which include discounts on bills, guaranteeing obligations and underwriting securities, and are hereinafter referred to as "loans, etc.") or equity-investments for the purpose of con- ducting projects deemed particularly important to contribute to the industrial development of developing countries and to promote economic interchange between the Republic of Korea and such countries (hereinafter referred to as "cooperation projects");

- Extending loans, etc. required to conduct investigations for the preparation of the cooperation projects or a trial-run of such projects;
- Extending loans, etc. required for the developing countries' importation of commodities deemed particularly important to stabilize the national economies of such countries from the Republic of Korea;
- Extending loans, etc. for projects conducive to the industrial development of developing countries and determined as such by Presidential Decree;
- Repayment of the principal of, and payment of the interest on, borrowings and deposits from the Public Capital Management Fund as referred to in the Public Capital Management Fund Act;
- Allocation for expenditures required for the creation, operation and management of the Fund.

4. Other Domestic Laws on the Korean ODA Activities

• Overseas Emergency Relief Act (2007)

The Overseas Emergency Relief Act covers the matters necessary for the Korean overseas emergency relief, such as dispatch of emergency relief teams, provision of emergency relief supplies, support for interim recovery from disasters, etc. In 2004 large-scale tsunami in South-Asia caused definite necessities and has had enough sympathy for legislating above, accordingly in 2007 finally all regarding act was announced to public.

According to the Act (Article 2), the term "overseas disaster" means a great deal of damage to property and physical suffering, which are caused by natural disasters, man-made disasters, other calamities or accidents in areas outside the territory of Korea. Furthermore, the term "overseas emergency relief" means all activities of providing emergency support to affected countries at governmental level, such as mitigation of or recovery from damage caused by overseas disasters, rescue of human lives, or medical relief work.

Article 1 of the Overseas Emergency Relief Act provides the purpose of the Act as below;

> *"The purpose of this Act is to contribute to providing rapid rescue and relief to disaster affected countries when overseas disasters occur, by prescribing the mat-*

ters necessary for overseas emergency relief, such as dispatch of emergency relief teams, provision of emergency relief supplies, support for interim recovery from disasters, etc."

The Overseas Emergency Relief Act consists of 18 articles and the main structure of the Act is below;

Article 1. Purpose
Article 2. Definitions
Article 3. Relationship with other Acts
Article 4. Basic Principle of Overseas Emergency Relief
Article 5. Types of Overseas Emergency Relief
Article 6. Establishment, etc. of Basic Measures for Overseas Emergency Relief
Article 6-2. stablishment of Health Care Activity System
Article 7. Commencement of Overseas Emergency Relief
Article 8. Public and Private Joint Council for Overseas Emergency Relief
Article 9. Consultation, etc. with Heads of Relevant Central Administrative Agencies
Article 10. Headquarters for Overseas Emergency Relief
Article 11. Organization and Dispatch of Overseas Emergency Relief Teams
Article 12. Captain of Overseas Emergency Relief Team

Article 13. Requests for Cooperation to Relevant Agencies
Article 14. Assistant to Participants in Overseas Emergency Relief
Article 15. Compensation, etc. for Participants in Overseas Emergency Relief
Article 16. Delegation and Entrustment of Authority
Article 17. Legal Fiction of Public Officials in Applying Penal Provisions

Article 6 of the Act provides that the Minister of Foreign Affairs shall establish basic measures for the overseas emergency relief activities. Then, the Minister shall notify the basic measures for overseas emergency relief to the heads of relevant central administrative agencies and have them implement the measures. Furthermore, the Minister shall report, each year, to the regular session of the National Assembly on the result of overseas emergency relief activities and the result of assessment.

Article 8 is on the Public and Private Joint Council for Overseas Emergency Relief activities. The article provides the operation of the public and private joint Council for overseas emergency relief in order to deliberate and pass resolutions on basic matters necessary to facilitate overseas emergency relief. The Council shall be chaired by the Minister of Foreign Affairs, and members of the Council shall be determined by Presidential Decree, from among vice minister-level public officials of relevant central administrative agencies, heads of relevant juristic persons and organizations, and experts in the relevant fields.

• Act on the Measures for the Admission to International Financial Institutions (1963)

Act on the Measures for the Admission to International Financial Institutions covers the membership with the international financial institutions and measures to discharge the responsibilities as a member prescribed in the agreements governing the respective international financial institutions. It is for discharging the responsibilities as a member prescribed in the agreements governing the respective international financial institutions. Article 1 of the Act provides the main purpose of the law as below;

> *"The purpose of this Act is to empower the Republic of Korea to take necessary measures to implement agreements with international financial institutions as a member of such international financial institutions."*

The volume of the Act is not so heavy. It just has several articles as below;

Article 1. Purpose
Article 2. Investment-related Institutions and Invest-

ment Funds

Article 3. Method of Investment

Article 4. Payment for Securities

Article 5. Delegates

Article 6. Depositary

Article 7. Deleted.

Article 2 provides the list of the 'Investment-related Institutions and Investment Funds' which is directly related to the Act. The term "international financial institution" in this Act means any of the following institutions;

- International Monetary Fund;
- International Bank for Reconstruction and Development;
- International Development Association;
- International Finance Corporation;
- Asian Development Bank;
- African Development Fund;
- African Development Bank;
- Common Fund for Commodities;
- Multilateral Investment Guarantee Agency;
- European Bank for Reconstruction and Development;
- Bank for International Settlements;
- Inter-American Development Bank;
- Inter-American Investment Corporation;

- Multilateral Investment Fund.
- Asian Infrastructure Investment Bank

If the government intends to make investments (including contribution) in an international financial institution from the list, a resolution by the National Assembly shall be obtained in advance. Then, the government shall endeavor to include investment funds in the budget, and where it is impracticable to do so due to a flexible response to financial circumstances and demand for investment, it may require the Bank of Korea to provide such investment funds. If the government requires the Bank of Korea to provide investment funds, it shall report the following matters to the National Assembly by September, 30 of each year.

Lecture 12.
The Law for KOICA

1. The Korea International Cooperation Agency (KOICA)

2. The KOICA Act

3. The Organisation of the KOICA (Article 8-14)

4. The Works of KOICA

The Law for KOICA

1. The Korea International Cooperation Agency (KOICA)

The Korea International Cooperation Agency (KOICA) was established as a government-funded agency dedicated to grant aid programs in 1991. Based on the KOICA Act declared in 1991, the agency has played a critical role in Korea's ODA platform. It endeavours to implement the government's grant aid and technical cooperation programmes in order to establish and strengthen socio-economic growth of developing countries.

Over the past 20 years until 2015, KOICA accounted for 45.51% of Korea's total spending in official development assistance. When it comes to grant aid only, KOICA accounted for 74.91% of the total national budget during the same period. KOICA operates one headquarter which consists of 10 departments, 8 offices, 28 teams, and 48 field offices around the globe as of September 2014. This organizational structure maximizes the effectiveness of Korea's grant aid programmes.

KOICA strives to meet the Basic Human Needs (BHNs) of developing countries and fostering their Human Resources Development (HRD). Recently, it has broadened to promote sustainable development, strengthening partnerships with developing partners, and enhancing the local ownership of beneficiaries. KOICA deals with global concerns of international community sector-wise, such as the environment, poverty reduction, and gender mainstreaming.

As Korea's ODA platform, KOICA is laying the foundation for stronger cooperation with domestic and international partners. In changing international trends, needs for the harmonisation between the trends and the Korean way has emerged. As the world has been globalized in which everyone on the globe share the universal values such as education, poverty, famine, civil rights, etc, realization on those values in global level became one of the main issues for developed countries. Korea, which has fruitful experiences on establishing fast socioeconomic development, is globally well known for its development model called 'Saemaul Undong.' KOICA is embarking on distributing this successful model to developing countries with some variation so that it would fit for its partner countries respectively.

In 2010, Korea became the 24th member of Development Assistance Committee (DAC) in OECD. Formerly learned, to become a member of DAC, one should meet a country's expenditure scale for ODA budget. Starting out as an agency of

KRW 18.6 billion, KOICA's budget skyrocketed to reach KRW 606.5 billion in 2014. The budget of KOICA is forecast to show a steady increase as Korea is expanding ODA to raise its ODA/GNI ratio to the level of OECD DAC average. Looking through title of regional departments in KOICA, it is implied that most of ODA from KOICA serves to countries in Asian region, followed by Africa and Latin America Department. Most of the proportion of grant aid disbursement goes to the Asia Pacific Ocean region, 63.2% as of 2014. Africa took 26.0% and Latin America took 10.8%.

KOICA expects that Korea's unique experience of developing from one of the poorest countries in the world to one of the most economically advanced would also be applied to other countries to be developed with support of various sectors. The know-how and experience Korea gained from the transition are invaluable assets that allow KOICA to efficiently support the sustainable socio-economic development of its partner countries and to offer them hope for a better world.

2. The KOICA Act

Align with Framework Act on International Development Cooperation, several agencies that support the basic ideologies and objectives speculated on the Act has established. KOICA is definitely one of them. As noted in Lecture 12 about domestic laws for Korean ODA, Framework Act has its upper position over KOICA act. The presidential decree of the Framework Act speculates that Minister of Foreign Affairs and chairperson of KOICA belong to CIDC. Based on the structure, KOICA became the subsidiary of MOFA, mainly being in charge of grants.

Article 1 of the KOICA Act provides that the purpose of this Act is, "To contribute to the promotion of international cooperation by establishing the Korea International Cooperation Agency and by having it perform various cooperative projects in order to promote the friendly and cooperative relationship and mutual exchange between the Republic of Korea and developing countries and assist the economic and social development of developing countries."

KOICA act defines several characteristics of the organization. To be noticeable in the act are fundamental purposes of the organization, legal personality, projects, the way it operates funds etc. By looking through related articles and paragraphs mentioned above, managerial structure and budget flow of ODA in Korea can be briefly shown. Also, specific tasks of the company are described on the Act. The Act consists of 31 Articles. The structure of the Articles of the Act is as listed below;

- Purpose
- Definition
- Legal Personality
- Establishment
- Establishment of Offices
- Articles of Association
- Projects
- Executives
- Grounds for Disqualification for Executives
- Duties of Executives
- Restrictions on Holding Concurrent Office by Executives and Employees
- Board of Directors
- Appointment and Dismissal of Employees
- Dispatch of Public Officials
- Operating Funds
- Contributions
- Gratuitous Loan of State Property
- Borrowing of Funds
- Contributors for International Antipoverty
- Report to the National Assembly
- Business Year
- Approval of Business Plan and Budget
- Submission of Settlement of Account

- Collection of Fees
- Direction and Supervision of Affairs
- Entrustment of Authority
- Affiliated Institutions
- Duty of Confidentiality
- Ban on Use of Similar Title
- Application of the Civil Act Mutatis Mutandis
- Legal Fiction as Public Officials in Application of Penal Provisions
- Penal Provisions
- Fines for Negligence

3. The Organisation of the KOICA (Article 8-14)

• Overview

Article 8 to Article 14 of the KOICA Act provides the details of the organisation of KOICA. Executives consist of the president, directors, and auditors. The president presides over a meeting of the board of directors. Departments and offices are classified by its regions and by its functions. In the headquarter in Korea, departments arrange according to its function have names of strategic planning, budget and legal affairs etc, whereas departments named after certain regional area focuses on localization and decentralization of development method for beneficiaries.

<Organisation of KOICA>

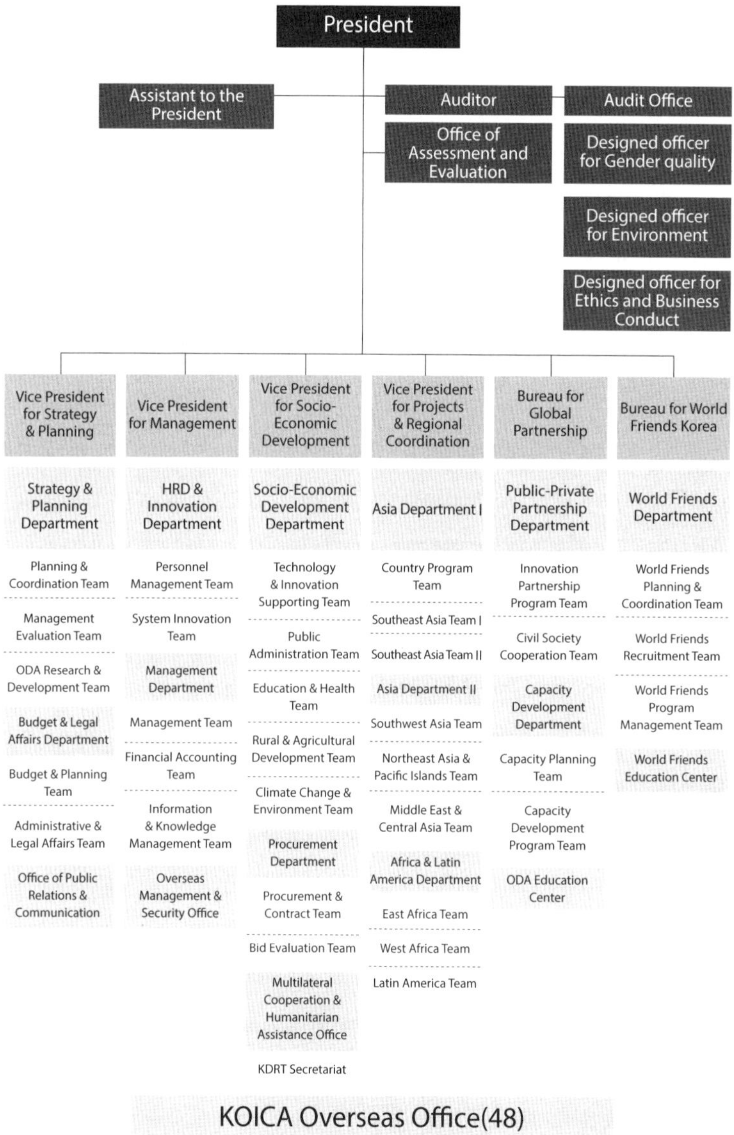

Source: http://www.koica.go.kr/ICSFiles/artimage/2015/07/06/cen105/con_organization.jpg

According to the articles, the structure of the organisation can be explained as below;

• **Executives**

Article 8 of the Act (Executives) provides various issues on the executives. According to the provisions, KOICA shall have 15 directors or fewer, including one Chairman and one auditor. Executives, other than the Chairman and standing directors prescribed by the articles of association, shall be non-standing executives. The Chairman of the agency shall be appointed by the President on the recommendation of the Minister of Foreign Affairs. Then, Directors (except ex officio directors prescribed by Presidential Decree) shall be appointed by the Minister of Foreign Affairs on the recommendation of the chairman. The auditor shall also be appointed by the Minister of Foreign Affairs. The term of office of the Chairman and directors shall be three years, the term of office of the auditor shall be two years and each of them may consecutively be reappointed for a second term only once.

Then, Article 9 provides the requirements for the executives with the reason of the disqualification for Executives as below;

No person who falls under any of the following subparagraphs shall be an executive of the Cooperation Agency:

- A non-national of the Republic of Korea;
- A minor;

- An incompetent of quasi-incompetent;
- A person declared bankrupt, but not yet reinstated;
- A person sentenced to imprisonment without prison labor or heavier punishment for whom three years have no yet elapsed since the execution of such sentence was completed or it was decided not to execute the sentence;
- A person who is disqualified or whose qualification is suspended pursuant to court judgement or other Acts.

Korean government strictly restricts any kind of commercial activities and exploitation of information gained from their official duties of the executives or the employees for the effectiveness and neutral position of the KOICA works. Article 11 (Restrictions on Holding Concurrent Office by Executives and Employees) shows the restrictions as below;

> The executives (excluding non-standing directors and the auditor; hereafter in this Article the same shall apply) and employees of the Cooperation Agency shall not engage in any profit-making business outside their duties, any executive shall not hold a concurrent office without permission of the Minister of Foreign Affairs and any employee without permission of the president.

4. The Works of KOICA

• The Theme of KOICA works

Based on Korea's Development Experience, KOICA sets the major development program by sector. The sectors are Public Administration, Education, Health, Rural Development, Industry and Energy, Cross-cutting Issues such as Environment, Gender, ICT, Human Rights. The details are as below;

Public Administration

To strengthen its support in the field of governance, KOICA developed the ODA Strategy for Governance (2011-2015) and set strategic objectives. Those strategic objectives include development of economic development strategy, establishment of e-government system, facilitation for efficient and transparent administration, construction of clear legal systems, etc

Education

KOICA is conducting education projects designed to expand education opportunities, upgrade the quality of education, and ensure access to education for all.

Health

Starting from dispatching medical workers to partner countries, it now increasingly focuses on building the capacity of the sector, increasing access to medical services, preventing and managing infectious diseases.

Rural Development

KOICA formulated KOICA Strategy on Agriculture and Fishery Development (2013-2015) to heighten the living standards and generate income for people living in rural areas. Particularly, in light of success of own nationwide development campaign 'Saemaul Undong', KOICA prepares to distribute the know-how of executing of the projects toward partner countries to increase people's well-being and eradicate poverty in rural regions

Industry and Energy

KOICA is implementing diverse development programmes aiming to establish infrastructures regarding transportation, energy or develop water resources.

Crosscutting Issues such as Environment, Gender, ICT, Human Rights

Other than 5 core sectors to focus, remaining themes are important in the view of common goals of international society are classified as crosscutting issues. KOICA spelled out the importance of the crosscutting issues such as environment and gender equality when developing its Mid-Term Advancement Plan (2011-2015).

• **The types of the works**

Article 7 of KOICA Act speculates the role of the organisation which is briefly summarised in 6 activities under the name of 'Projects'. They are training, dispatch of experts, development studies, infrastructure support, partnerships with International institutions and NGOs, emergency relief. Specific methods of some activities are additionally stated in other articles. The provision is as shown below;

> In order to achieve the purposes referred to in Article 1. the Cooperation Agency shall carry out the following projects:
>
> The following projects for developing countries:
> - Invitation of trainees;
> - Dispatch of professional human resources;
> - Dispatch of Korea Overseas Volunteers;
> - Research in development;
> - Disaster relief;
> - Assistance with goods, funds and facilities;
>
> The following projects for international cooperation:
> - Support to international cooperation activities of non-governmental organisations;
> - Cooperation with foreign aid-related organisations

and international organisations;

- Research and study on the formulation of ideologies and policies on international cooperation;
- Other projects necessary for the promotion of international cooperation;

Projects entrusted by Government;

Education and training, publicity and other projects incidental to projects under subparagraphs 1 through 3.

For the works, KOICA may request any State agency through the Minister of Foreign Affairs to dispatch public officials, if necessary to achieve its purposes. Then, head of a State agency upon receipt of the request may dispatch public officials under his/her control to the Cooperation Agency.

• The work schemes

KOICA has invented its own development programmes through many years of ODA, which finally categorised into 7 activities by type as of 2015. Those programmes are; Projects and DEEP, World Friends Korea, Fellowship Programme CIAT, Humanitarian Assistance and Disaster Relief, Civil Society Cooperation, ODA Education Research Evaluation, Grant Aid and Aid Procurement. These programmes can find its reason to run on basis of KOICA act.

Projects and DEEP

KOICA is conducting the Development Experience and Exchange Program (DEEP) as a means of technical cooperation to build the capacity of partner countries by sharing Korea's development experience. It is one of the leading programmes of KOICA. In addition, KOICA took on vocational training programs and sericulture assistance programs in association with Ministries of Korean government.

World Friends Korea

There has been always a need to integrate government's overseas volunteer programs hosted by several ministries. 'World Friends Korea' became the initiative that managed and supervised all the volunteer dispatch programs since 2009.

Fellowship Program CIAT Partnerships with NGOs

CIAT, is an abbreviated word for Capacity Improvement and Advancement for Tomorrow, also has a meaning of 'seed' that implies generally 'hope for future' in Korean. It is KOICA's global training program that aims to share development experience and know-how with public officials from partner countries through invitational training.

Humanitarian Assistance and Disaster Relief

KOICA carried several relief activities in case of natural disasters such as earthquakes, typhoons, and tsunamis, etc. In particular in 2013, KOICA dispatched Korean Disaster Relief Team to the region stroke by typhoon in 'Haiyan', providing more than 6,000 medical services to local residents.

Civil Society Cooperation

Civil Society Cooperation Project is the participatory development project that engages with private sector partners such as civil society organizations, businesses and universities.

ODA Education-Research-Evaluation

KOICA operates education and research programs in partnership with NGOs, civic group. Its prime subject is diversifying aid channels and training future generation of global cooperation leaders. Also, ODA evaluation is taken on on-going or completed project based on OECD DAC assessment criteria.

Grant Aid Program & Aid Procurement

KOICA created a department dedicated to aid procurement to develop expertise, establish a platform for procurement information delivery and meet international norms in aid procurement.

Lecture 13.
The Law for EDCF

1. The Law for the EDCF Works by Korea Eximbank
2. The Economic Development Cooperation Fund of Korea
3. Roles of EDCF - Types and the Procedures under the Act
4. The Loan Procedure in the Bank

The Law for EDCF

1. The Law for the EDCF Works by Korea Eximbank

• The Korea Export-Import Bank

Korea Export-Import Bank was established in 1976. It mainly acts as official Export Credit Agency of Republic of Korea (ECA). Therefore the credit level of Korea recognized by global society is the same as that of Korea Eximbank. This credit level influences Korean businesspeople who runs international business company and foreign companies which would try to do business with Korean companies. In order to support Korean enterprises in conducting overseas business, Korea Eximbank, as an ECA of Republic of Korea, provides export credit and guarantee programmes to domestic companies.

The bank has been always along with the Korea's policies for the export-led economy and economic cooperation with foreign countries. Financial service they provide mainly focuses on facilitation of exporting; it deals with export loans, trade finance, and guarantee programmes as other national trade finance banks in other countries does. Besides, the bank especially operates 2 government funds; the Economic Development Cooperation Fund (EDCF) for ODA, and the Inter-Korean Cooperation Fund (IKCF) for economic cooperation with North Korea.

• The Korea Export-Import Bank Act

The Korea Export-Import Bank Act which is the foundation of the bank's operation comprises of 42 Articles and 5 Chapters. With the basic act of 42 articles, enforcement decree which provides details on executing the 42 articles is also declared. Article 1 of the Act provides the purpose of the Act as: "to promote the sound development of the national economy by providing finance required for the overseas economic cooperation, such as export and import, overseas investment and exploitation of overseas resources or such through the incorporation of the Export-Import Bank of Korea."

The bank is a juristic person and operated as prescribed by this Act. Therefore, the Bank of Korea Act, the Banking Act, and Act on Ruling System of Financial Companies shall not apply to the bank. Structure of Korea Export-Import Bank Act is as below;

Chapter 3. Duties

Article 18. Duties

Article 19. Deleted

Article 19-2. Guarantee for Borrowing of Foreign Capital

Article 20. Export and import finance bond

Article 20-2. Investment, etc. to Juristic Persons

Article 21. Application for approval of Operational plans

Article 22. Deleted

Article 23. Limited amount of loan, etc.

Article 24. Cooperation with other Financial Institutions

Article 25. Restriction on Business

Article 26. Interest rate on Loan and Discount, and Rates for Guarantee fees

Article 27. Restriction on property ownership

Article 28. Vicarious Performance of Duties

Article 29. Operational Manual

Article 30. Deleted

Chapter 4. Finance and Accounting

Article 31. Business year

Article 32. Budget

Article 33. Revised supplementary Budget

Article 34. Reserve fund

Article 35. Settlement of Accounts

Article 36. Disposal Profits

Article 37. Compensation for Amount of Loss

Article 38. Use of Surplus Funds

Chapter 5. Supplementary Provision

Article 39. Supervision

Article 40. Reasons for Dismissal of Executives

Article 41. Report and Inspection

Article 41-2. Special Cases concerning Investment under Special Acts

Article 42. Administrative Fines

Article 43. Deleted

• The Roles of the Bank

One of the roles of Korea Eximbank is an ECA (Export Credit Agency) facilitating export transactions. It provides export credits to promote the export of capital goods such as ships and industrial plants and high technology industries such as IT. It also provides credits to support overseas investments, overseas projects, and natural resource development projects

Korea Eximbank acts as an executor of EDCF (Economic Development Cooperation Fund) enhancing cooperative ties with developing countries. EDCF under Korea Eximbank appraises loan agreements and implements evaluation for economic development aid projects in developing countries. It also acts as an executor of IKCF (Inter-Korean Cooperation Fund) contributing to the foundation for reunification of North and South Korea. IKCF

Serves as a clearing settlement bank with the Foreign Trade Bank of North Korea.

It also launches research on ODA (Official Development Assistance) policy directions. Overseas Economic Research Institute under Korea Eximbank appraises, disburses, and provides ex-post management for grants and loans regarding the fund

2. The Economic Development Cooperation Fund of Korea

• The Economic Development Cooperation Fund (EDCF)

As explained above, there are 2 cooperation fund which is operated for other than domestic regions. One is the Economic Development Cooperation Fund, the other is the Inter-Korean Cooperation Fund (IKCF). Since the EDCF takes part in most of finance of Korean ODA. This section mainly covers information on EDCF as the representative finance of Korean ODA.

Korea established the Economic Development Cooperation Fund (EDCF) in 1987 with the purpose of promoting economic cooperation between Korea and developing countries. Drawing on Korea's own development experience over the years, the EDCF assists partner countries by providing funding for their industrial development and economic stability. The fund is concentrating on capacity building of partner countries, with the goal to help them achieve self-reliance.

For this purpose, the main areas of assistance are human resources and economic infrastructure. Specifically in the area of human resource development, Korea has committed not only providing educational equipment for developing countries, but also sharing the lessons it has learned from decades of development experience through operating various trainee and expert exchange programs. In terms of economic infrastructure assistance the fund has assisted partners in their development of the information technology (IT) industry. There is more room for participation by innovative small and medium-sized enterprises.

• Economic Development Cooperation Fund (EDCF) Act

Align with Framework Act on International Development Cooperation, several agencies that support the basic ideologies and objectives speculated on the Act has established. EDCF is definitely one of them. As noted in Lecture 12 about domestic laws for Korean ODA, Framework Act has its upper position over EDCF act. The presidential decree of the Framework Act speculates that Minister of Strategy and Finance and chairperson of Korea Eximbank belong to CIDC. Based on the structure, Korea Eximbank is entrusted by government of the operation of the Fund in association with MOSF which is responsible for the overall management of EDCF.

The EDCF Act is the special law for the establishment and the management of the funds. Rationale on foundation of EDCF is based on the Act firstly enforced on in 1987, renewed up until on 1st March, 2016. It has 15 Articles with a Presidential Decree. The provisions are mainly related to the fund such as Establishment and Financial Sources; Use, Operation and Management; Requirement for Assistance and Accounting Agency. Furthermore, the law has other provisions on other matters regarding the fund such as Long-term and temporary borrowings; Disposition of profit and loss and Supervision and order by the authority.

Article 1. Purpose
Article 2. Definitions
Article 3. Establishment of Fund
Article 4. Financial Sources of Fund
Article 5. Long-term Borrowings
Article 6. Deleted
Article 7. Use of Fund
Article 8. Requirement for Assistance from Fund
Article 9. Operation and Management of Fund
Article 10. Fund Management Council
Article 11. Temporary Borrowings
Article 12. Use of Surplus Funds
Article 13. Accounting Agency of Fund
Article 14. Disposition of Profit and Loss

Article 15. Supervision and Order

• Funding Resources and use of the Fund

Article 4 the Act specifies the resources of the fund. Basically, the 6 main resources are as below:

- Contributions by the Government;
- Contributions by public institutions under the Act on the Management of Public Institutions prescribed by Presidential Decree, or economic organizations;
- Contributions from other government funds;
- Long-term borrowings pursuant to Article 5;
- Deposits from the Public Capital Management Fund as referred to in the Public Capital Management Fund Act;
- Profits from the operation of the Fund

According to the Article 5, the Minister of Strategy and Finance may, when it is deemed necessary, incur long-term debts from other funds, banks, foreign governments, foreign financial institutions, international financial organisations, etc. at the expense of the Fund, in order to raise funds for the Fund.

Then, Article 7 provides that the Fund is operated for the following purposes:

- Extending loans or equity-investments for the purpose of conducting projects deemed particularly important to contribute to the industrial development of developing countries and to promote economic interchange between Korea and such countries (cooperation projects)
- Extending loans, etc. required to conduct investigations for the preparation of the cooperation projects or a trial-run of such projects
- Extending loans, etc. required for the developing countries' importation of commodities deemed particularly important to stabilize the national economies of such countries from Korea
- Extending loans, etc. for projects conducive to the industrial development of developing countries and determined as such by Presidential Decree
- Coverage for loss in case where the loan interest cannot cover the cost of the implementation intended for developing countries
- Repayment of the principal of, and payment of the interest on, borrowings and deposits from the Public Capital Management Fund as referred to in the Public Capital Management Fund Act
- Allocation for expenditures required for the creation, operation and management of the Fund.

• **EDCF and the Bank**

Article 9 of the Act describes the administrative operation and management of the EDCF. According to the provision, the Minister of Strategy and Finance shall operate and manage the Fund. Furthermore, the Minister may entrust the Export-Import Bank of Korea with business concerning the operation and management of the Fund, as prescribed by Presidential Decree.

In practice, the Fund Management Council composed of 12 members, most of whom are ministerial-level government officials is the highest policy-making authority of the EDCF. Then, the direction of EDCF operations and the assumption of principal policy-making responsibilities rest with the Ministry, which also coordinates policy matters with other relevant ministries. Entrusted by the Ministry, the Korea Eximbank is the practical administrative operator of the fund. The bank runs the procedures for the management of the fund including appraisal of project, execution of the loan agreements, and loan disbursements. Other duties include principal/interest payments collection, project supervision, and ex-post evaluation of project operations.

Other services they provide regarding extension of its loans are: principal/interest payments collection, project supervision, ex-post evaluation of project operations, and advisory services.

3. Roles of EDCF - Types and the Procedures under the Act

• Types of Loans

There are several types of the loans categorized by subjects, objects and main targets.

- Development Project Loan is used for infrastructure projects, such as construction of roads, railways, hospitals, vocational training canters, and water supply
- Equipment Loan provides funds to procure equipment for the national development plan
- Public-Private Partnership (PPP) Loan provides funds to conduct Public (governments)–Private (corporations) Partnership projects.
- Two-Step Loan provides funds to make sub-loans through the financial institutions for the implementation of designated policies. It is usually utilized to promotion of small and medium sized enterprises in specified industries.
- Commodity Loan provides funds to import commodities for the economic stabilisation of partner country

• Terms and Conditions of the Loans

Basically EDCF classifies developing countries into five categories for assignment of the interest rate and repayment period. Criteria are given with consideration to the phase of economic development, per capita income levels, and other relevant factors.

In general, once the organization starts review on executing loans for certain project, amount of loan is decided upon the total project cost. Interest Rate of the loan ranges from 0.01 to 2.5% per annum, which is relatively much lower than any other private finance. Repayment period reaches up to 40 years. Repayment period is set to come semi-annually.

4. The Loan Procedure in the Bank

• Details on the Procedure

Policy dialogue: To determine a project's feasibility, economic and technical aspects must be closely examined. Feasibility studies may be carried out either by the governments of partner countries or multilateral organizations such as the World Bank and the ADB, or with technical assistance from donor countries. If the government of a partner country requires assistance in preparing for a project that will be financed through EDCF loans, it may also request assistance from Korea Eximbank or the Korean government to carry out preparations

Project Preparation: Partner countries prepare feasibility

<EDCF Loan Procedure Overview>

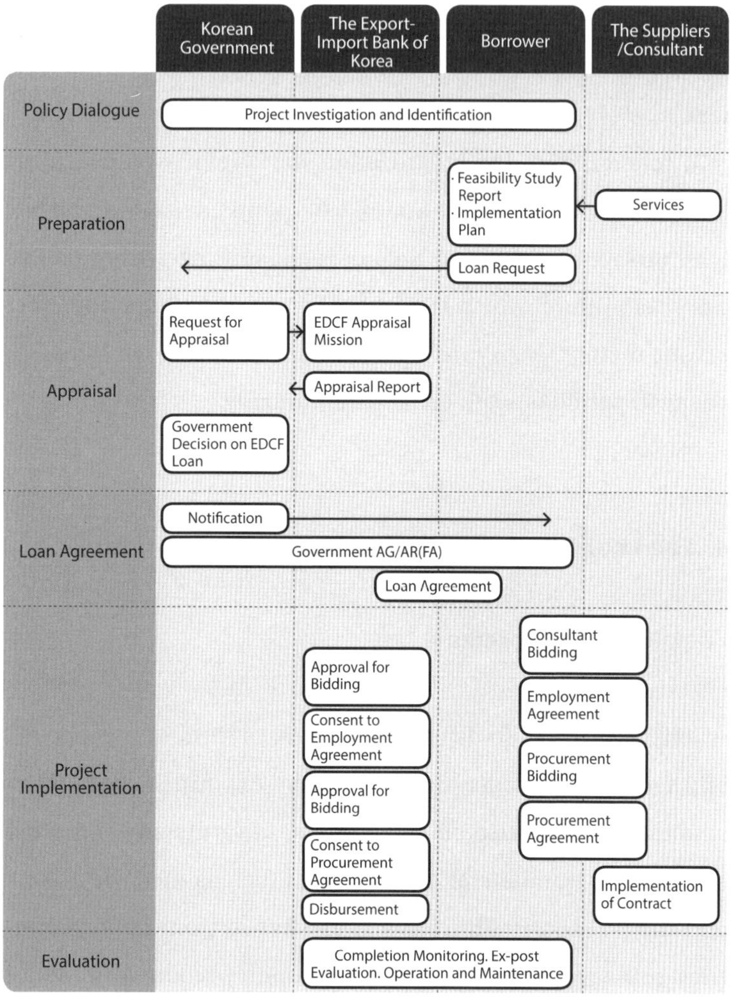

<Korea Eximbank, 2015, "Guide to EDCF", p.18-29>

studies for candidate projects for EDCF loans. To request EDCF loans, several documents must be submitted to the Korean government. Those are loan requests, feasibility studies report, and implementation plans. Partner countries forward those documents to the Korean embassies in their territory. Then the minister of MOFA notifies the Minister of MOSF of the requests

Appraisal: After receiving the loan request, MOSF makes a preliminary decision on to extend the EDCF loan, based on its review on project documents. Document is evaluated by several yardsticks such as project's contribution to industrial development or economic stabilization. If the project is deemed suitable, MOSF requests that Korea Eximbank conducts project appraisal. After Korea Eximbank completes the appraisal report and submits it along with its opinion to MOSF, MOSF confirms the economic, financial, ad technical soundness of the project based on Korea Eximbank's appraisal report. After discussion with the ministries concerned, MOSF makes a final decision on the loan request and notifies the partner country through MOFA.

Loan Agreement: Prior to drafting a Loan Agreement, Korea Eximbank sends the partner country a legally binding questionnaire to determine the legal background related to the loan. When loan negotiations are completed and the specific terms and conditions are agreed upon, a Loan Agreement is signed between Korea Eximbank and the partner country.

Project Implementation: Once the Loan Agreement is signed, the project is implemented by the Project Executing Agency (PEA) according to the agreed schedule and procedures.

Evaluation: Korea Eximbank conducts Completion Monitoring and Ex-post Evaluation after a project implementation is concluded. The main reason for conducting evaluation is to improve the quality of EDCF assistance and to ensure accountability and transparency of the whole process.

- **Recent projects carried by EDCF**

Korea-Myanmar Friendship Bridge Project

After reinitiating its support to Myanmar in 2011, EDCF has actively identified new projects through summit meetings, Korea-Myanmar Economic Cooperation Council and Policy Dialogues. In 2014, the Framework Arrangement (F/A) was established, indicating full-fledged support is to be given in the years to come. The Korea-Myanmar Friendship (Dala) Bridge Project, approved in December 2014, is the largest EDCF project that has been implemented in Myanmar, with total commitments amounting to USD 137.8 million. The project consists of the construction of a 2.5km long cable-stayed bridge and its approach roads. For the successful project implementation, EDCF loan will be used for the procurement of goods and services required for the construction of the bridge, technology transfer training, and consulting services on, for example, detailed design and bid preparation. The bridge is expected to drastically improve the transportation environment around the Yangon river, heavily dependent on waterborne transportation such as ferries. It will also be able to meet the increasing transport demands resulting from the city's rapid economic growth. In addition, the bridge will contribute to the balanced development between Yangon and Dala by promoting personal, physical and economic exchanges, which leads to the improvement of the quality of life in the Dala region. The Korea-Myanmar Friendship Bridge, the first bridge that crosses the Yangon river, is expected to become a national landmark which symbolizes Korea's contribution through ODA and will enhance EDCF's global reputation. For these reasons, this project plays a crucial role in strengthening mutual cooperation and friendship between Korea and Myanmar.

Ambulance and Firefighting Equipment Supply Project in Mozambique

Mozambique, located in the south-east of Africa, is one of the fastest growing economies in Africa. However, rapid economic growth brought huge inflows of population into the cities, increasing crimes and the homeless. Hence, there is a rising need for protecting the safety and properties of the people. The government of Mozambique has established the Emergency Management Informational System Master Plan which aims at achieving Safe Mozambique by 2017. As part of such efforts, the Emergency Management Information System Project (EMIS) has been implemented to protect people's lives and properties, requiring more specialized firefighting equipment to be used.

Furthermore, the Mozambique government has developed the Strategic Plan for Health Sector which contains the plan to strengthen and improve hospital referral networks that connect five main hospitals for emergency patient transport. To do so, fully equipped ambulances are highly needed to efficiently connect with key hospitals in emergency situations. As a reply to the request from the Mozambique government, EDCF approved the Compact Loan in December 2014 for Mozambique to acquire 21 fire trucks with firefighting accessories attached, and 45 ambulances with medical devices installed. EDCF will also provide on-site training for the effective use of the equipment in Mozambique. The Mozambique government expects that the project will prevent accidents and diseases, and improve the general quality of life of the people in Mozambique.